PRAISE FOR SOULCATIC

“*Soulcation* is a much-needed floatat[illegible] something to hang onto as you figure out how to hear your voice while swimming in a sea of all the others. The bonus is that it will also bring you to shore.”

–Steph Jagger, world record holder and author of *Everything Left to Remember* and *Unbound*

“What *Soulbbattical* is for corporate rebels, *Soulcation* is going to be for the generation of millennials itching for more.”

–Shelley Paxton, former CMO of Harley Davidson and author of *Soulbbatical: A Corporate Rebel’s Guide to Finding Your Best Life*

“This book is mandatory reading for anyone looking for more freedom and joy in their life (especially their work life). Mel turned her own personal story into actionable life design tools that go far beyond ‘self-help.’ It’s not just cookie-cutter solutions: this book will transform the way you think about purpose and give you a clear roadmap to design a life you don’t need a vacation from.”

–Allison Fallon, author of The Power of Writing it Down

“For anyone struggling with burnout – and at some point in their lives, that’s EVERYONE – this book is for you. It will inspire you to choose yourself, reprioritize what’s most important, and truly build a life that makes you happy.”

–Lauren Smith, author of *The Mindful Dating Journal: Find A Healthy Love That Lasts*

"*Soulcation* is not just a memoir: it's a beautiful permission slip on how to build a life you love. In a time where hustle is praised and yet we're all suffering from overwork Mel offers a new and refreshing way to pursue what truly matters. This book is the medicine for anyone who feels burdened by a life of expectations and is looking to design a satisfying and joyful life."

–Kara Elise Campbell, embodiment coach, creator of the Embodiment Deck, and former celebrity chef

"*Soulcation* is the book we all desperately need right now! In this world where we all seem to be on a treadmill that has some dude (or dudette) slyly pushing the 'Up' button every day, Mel provides a way to run on that treadmill in a totally different way. If you're burnt out, fed up, or let down, *Soulcation* will show you the way up and out!"

–Erin Hatzikostas, author of *You Do You(ish)*, TEDx speaker, and founder of b Authentic Inc.

"By doing everything I thought I should be doing, I hustled myself into anxiety and overwhelm. Mel's book combines relatable stories with real strategies to take back your life. She cracks open her soul and leads us on a personal journey for real change. We don't need fancy vacations to find peace and joy. We just need a little more *Soulcation*."

–Renee Bauer, Founder of Happy Even After

"*Soulcation* is a compelling guide and inspiring reminder that life is meant to be fully lived. Americans are so programmed to hustle and rush that we often lose sight that joy in life is found in the simple sacred moments. Mel offers us not only a guide for how to live a life you don't need a vacation from but parts of her sacred story. What a gift she has given us."

–Britt Ross, holistic health writer and CEO of Mission108

"In *Soulcation*, Mel combines heart and soul with the mind of a scientist, inspiring you to experiment with your life in a way that society discourages. She teaches you it's okay to start over, to choose yourself, to rest instead of work, and to listen to your own voice in a world trying to drown you out. This book will drastically change the way you think about what you want, how to get there, and what will make you happy. This book will also help you unlearn the pain-inducing patterns you've been conditioned to run. Simply put, *Soulcation* will change your life."

–Connell Barrett, dating coach, bestselling author of *Dating Sucks but You Don't*, and founder of DatingTransformation.com

"This book is a SOULution to your unconscious habits and patterns that lead to exhaustion. The deep fatigue that so many working women feel is not only from pushing hard, but from lack of attunement with themselves: their grief, needs, and desires. Mel Miles has both lived a path back to connection and wholehearted living, and offered an inner and outer map for the journey. We need more women courageous enough to ditch the old maps and mindsets that were handed to us, and create and share new ones."

–Whitney Otto, Performance and Executive Coach.

"Our lives feel full, maybe too full sometimes, right? But we look away from the cracks when they appear ... sleep is off, we're eating poorly, drinking a bit too much, running late all the time, and the weight on our chest when the boss wants it now should really worry us. In a vulnerable and honest voice Mel Miles asks us to stop and observe before it's too late. *Soulcation* is an answer to a question we aren't ready to ask – could I live differently and still have what makes me happy?"

–Patti Hall, author of *Loving Large*

"The people we meet and books we read are the primary agents of change in our lives. Meet Mel Miles through her refreshing book, *Soulcation,* and continue your journey forward."

–Arnie Malham, Founder of BetterBookClub

SOUL
CATION

SOUL CATION

Design a Life You Don't Need a Vacation From

End Burnout, Unwind Anxiety, and Become Wildly Free in a Culture Addicted to Busy

Mel Miles

The events and conversations in this book have been set down to the best of the author's ability, although some names and details have been changed to protect the privacy of individuals.

First paperback edition April 2022

Book design by Morgane Leoni
Cover design by Josefina Nino

ISBN 979-8-9858531-8-6 (paperback)

ISBN 979-8-9858531-3-1 (ebook)

www.takeasoulcation.com

To my mother, who whispered in my ear as she was dying, "You should write a book."

TABLE OF CONTENTS

LOVE LETTER FROM MEL

We always think we have things figured out. That is, until life brings us another shitshow. The cycle of stability, chaos, and rebirth I now am able to see is a portal taking us deeper into love. But one of the scariest feelings in the world is when shit hits the fan and we don't (yet) know how to get through it. This book is a love letter to that feeling.

The writing of this book started with my personal rock-bottom. I was hospitalized for a panic attack, one that happened on the heels of my mother's death, the sudden end of my marriage, and the worst anxiety I'd experienced in a decade-long battle with it. Despite what looked like success—working for the Bill & Melinda Gates Foundation, meeting with heads of state, standing in my feminist power—on the inside it felt like anything but success. My adult acne, god-awful headaches, chronic back pain, and reliance on caffeine and alcohol only added to the stress, anxiety, and exhaustion. It was arguably inevitable I would end up in the dreaded yet all-too-common state: burnout.

Quitting my job was the only thing I KNEW FOR CERTAIN I wanted to do amidst the chaos. So with a faint hope of finding relief, I left my home, sold most of my belongings, and set out with my scientific training to study how women can optimize life for their own happiness. To arrive at the concept of Soulcation, I interviewed women from over a dozen countries, walked the Camino de Santiago solo across Spain, studied meditation (including eight days in complete silence), did ayahuasca in the Mexican jungle, and experimented with both Eastern and Western healing techniques, including medication, therapy, psychodrama, water therapy, ecstatic dance therapy, herbalism, yoga, and tantra. I explored happiness from a place of desperately wanting to find it for myself, as an average person, with an average savings account, and an average middle-class, American upbringing.

Originally I thought Soulcation might be another *Eat, Pray, Love* story. But what I discovered was the magic of Soulcation had nothing to do with me leaving. It wasn't the plane tickets I bought or Airbnbs that healed me. Rather, the magic of my "Pause" was that it gave me a glimpse of a new lifestyle, one where I could see, smell, taste, and even feel in my body what I couldn't for the three decades before: the possibility of doing the things I used to only do on vacation in my everyday life.

It was a slow awakening. Rather than my usual mojo of fighting harder as the chaos increased, the days I spent traveling, walking, sitting in stillness, and sharing meals with diverse people around the world were my gateway to a path of ease. The extra time and space in my life gave me a chance to ask: *What if life could be easy? And what if this feeling of ease and softness could be the compass for how I guide my life?*

As the universe would have it, as I emerged from my Pause and was about to write this book, another shitstorm hit: COVID-19. I had plans to continue traveling the world as a digital nomad, living in vacation cities, working remotely, and jumping from one adventure to the next. However, in the wake of COVID-19 something I didn't expect happened: I didn't miss traveling. In fact, I started to crave rootedness, consistency, and stability. I wanted the spaciousness, simplicity, and fun from my vacation lifestyle, but I wanted my own bed, my own set of clay mugs to drink my morning coffee from, and some plants to call my own. So in the early days of lockdown, I started deploying everything I had learned about

Soulcation (although it didn't have this name yet). I made a list of the things I loved to do on vacation, gave myself permission to act in alignment with my energy (rather than my calendar), created shorter work-from-home workdays, and scripted with great detail the daily rhythms of rest, work, and play I wanted. The challenges of the pandemic became the testing ground for the concepts I was writing in this book.

And while no one can deny the tragedy, stress, and sadness that the pandemic unleashed on our world, these years have served as a growth opportunity–and with the tools that I learned (and that I'll teach you), these years within a new world have been some of the best of my life. I was able to claim new self-care habits, take back control of my time, and experience vacation vibes on a daily basis, without getting on a single plane. As of fall 2021, I have settled into a new home, job, and routine in Lisbon, Portugal, where I moved to ensure I could Soulcation long-term.

While I have experienced a beautiful rebirth from the shitshow documented in this book, the truth is it took me four years, all my savings, and a lot of failed attempts to arrive here. I wrote this book as a love letter to anyone else weathering a storm. May ***Soulcation*** make your inevitable journey through the shitshow smoother and full of ease.

Mel Miles
March 8, 2022

INTRODUCTION

We've been told a lie. And if we're honest, we're all part of a generation living in the wake of this lie. I tell you this not to be blunt, but because your happiness literally depends on it, and I wrote this book to help you spend more time feeling happy.

It's a myth that our busy calendars, workaholic lifestyles, and hustle-hard mindsets will make us feel the way we want to feel. I suspect your body already knows this is true, and you're holding this book because you crave relief from the low energy, chronic stress, and/or anxiety you just can't seem to outrun. If you feel this way, please take it as mere evidence you are human in the twenty-first century. Our ability to slow down, relearn rhythms of rest, and manage our energy (not our Google calendars) is inevitably the challenge of our generation, whether we consciously accept it or not.

The irony of writing a book about how to bring vacation energy into everyday life is not lost on me. We are among the richest generations in American history. We have spent the most money on vacations than any other humans to have walked the planet. Simultaneously, economic inequality is at an all-time high, and going on more vacations is not an option for many. Even among those who manage to take time off work, we have the highest rates of anxiety and depression ever reported, feel the least amount of connection and love in our relationships, and hospice interviews show that most of us will die with the regret that we never gave ourselves permission to spend more time on the things that make us happy. There are countless apps and demands for our attention, a nebulous divide between our home and work life, and still a lingering and unspoken expectation that we women, in particular, will sacrifice our sleep or time for ourselves to make the family or work calendar... well, work. We have almost unconsciously allowed our energy tank to hover near empty. And then when shit hits the fan, we keep telling ourselves, "Life is supposed to be hard," and keep pushing through.

But what if you could stop checking off everything on your lists *and* feel much more ecstatic, satisfied, and full of joy? Soulcation is based on the belief it is our birthright for life to be wild, free, and full of ease. It addresses the problem that somewhere along the line we started to believe we had to earn these feelings, and that slowness will not lead to success; intuition and energy are not trustworthy signals; and it's selfish to give ourselves exactly what we need, want, and desire. So we went on trusting our calendars, our bosses, and our one- and five-year plans, without ever stopping to ask ourselves if there was an entirely different way to live.

If you don't believe it's possible to create a life dripping with fun, pleasure, and happiness within the constructs of your current circumstances, I wrote this book for you. Why? Because I was once the biggest skeptic out there. I didn't believe I could trust the path of ease, let alone arrive at a sustained place of happiness before I achieved everything I was working towards.

I now know the Soulcation method works because I've used it to transform my own life. As a public health expert for some of the most influential billionaires in human history (Bill and Melinda Gates) I spent years working sixty hours a week. I traveled to over twenty-five African countries before I was thirty-three years old. On the outside, I had so much. And yet on the inside, I was always anxious about the future, addicted to managing my calendar to the quarter-hour and found that no matter how much "success" I achieved, I still never felt satisfied. I was unconvinced it was really possible to live wildly free. However, when my lifelong battle with anxiety finally left me hospitalized, I had no choice but to reckon with my skepticism and reach for tools I hadn't tried yet. This book tells the story of the tools that helped me transform, and how I radically changed my mind about the achievability of happiness along the way.

WE ARE ALL BURNED OUT

It's not just you. Burnout is all around us. What we perceive as digestive issues, skin conditions, headaches, heart problems, diabetes, asthma, immune diseases, chronic pain, and arthritis (to name a few), have all been strongly linked to how stress and emotional fatigue manifest in our nervous systems. Despite this evidence, we usually only admit something is wrong when a life crisis hits: divorce, job loss, serious diagnosis, or whatever cocktail of rock-bottom the universe serves up. Then we act surprised about how seriously these life transitions are impacting us. Yet no matter if your breaking point comes through being hospitalized from burnout (like I was), or in the early stages of misalignment where you simply feel "meh" about something (a much easier place to do life design work from and why you should read this book cover to cover now), at some point we all have to come to terms with choices that earlier versions of ourselves made (saying yes to a job, relationship, or home) that are now not aligned, and have us on a path of stress. The work of Soulcation is to trust those emotional and physical cues enough to try new tools, and take fresh action.

DESIGN A LIFE YOU DON'T NEED A VACATION FROM

What does it look like to Soulcation?

Let's start by allowing your mind to enter a new scene. Imagine being so in charge of your time that you don't always set an alarm. When you wake up, you have scrapped that old gym routine that felt like misery and instead you savor a morning ritual chock-full of things you love and that bring you energy. You check in with your energy (asking yourself how you are feeling emotionally and physically) and structure your day accordingly. Then imagine you have so much clarity on your work priorities you only need to work four to six hours a day (yes, this could be at your same job, with your same salary). You now have one or two extra hours in the day to spend on something for yourself: pursuing a hobby, launching a dream project, picking up a new sport. This time for YOU becomes so consistent and ingrained that you now make it a practice to schedule your rest and play with the same level of effort and gusto as you used to schedule your work tasks. And rather than beating yourself up each New Year's with the next unattainable weight loss or work goal, you make an annual "Happy List" of things that would add more pleasure or adventure to your life. Imagine how many wild dreams you might pursue or places in the world you might go if you gave yourself permission.

This, my friends, is what Soulcation is all about. It's not about booking a ticket to the Bahamas or finding a way to take more vacations. It's about connecting with the vacation version of yourself (the one that's open to new people, new possibilities, new ideas, and new fun) in your everyday life.

I know. You might be thinking, *how can I possibly do this while still fulfilling my responsibilities as an adult?* I wrote this book to prove it's much easier than you think. It doesn't require you to be rich, kid-free, or run your own business. I've lived a Soulcation life while having a traditional nine-to-five job, on less than half my previous salary, and with only a suitcase's worth of possessions. Living a life you don't need a vacation from is not about ignoring responsibilities, dropping the ball, or recklessly spending your money on yourself. The methods I teach in *Soulcation* are all about becoming a student of your own happiness, so you can tend to your own needs as much as you do everyone else's.

WHAT YOU WILL LEARN IN THIS BOOK

This book is part teaching, part memoir. I've structured it this way because I believe story is the most powerful teacher, and life is best lived when we start to see ourselves as the heroines of our own stories. In the pages that follow you will read about the most shameful, painful, and downright embarrassing moments of my journey from burnout to living the Soulcation lifestyle. Even my best friends questioned whether I should publish some of the things inside these pages. But my gut told me pulling back that curtain on my own four-year recovery would help ease the pain as you travel your own rocky and beautiful path.

Since I'm a public health expert and scientist by training, the book brings in my knowledge from working on public health programs for the Bill & Melinda Gates Foundation, U.S. Centers for Disease Control, and World Health Organization to teach Soulcation in a way that is practical, replicable, and results in impact.

Part I ("Burnout") dives deep into the research and belief systems that lead to stress and burnout. We introduce the stages of burnout along with the role internalized capitalism–the belief that our self-worth is directly linked to our productivity–plays in its progression. We also discuss why even though we know a habit isn't good for us it's so hard to change; why we stay busy and keep checking all the boxes but our own; and the lies we believe about work, happiness, and vacation.

In Part II ("What it Takes to Soulcation") we go deep into the invisible inner work required to design a life you don't need a vacation from. This includes the neuroscience of how we numb negative emotions; the gentle (vacation-like) pathway you can use to turn toward your emotional pain and trauma; and how to train your mind to trust your body, your feelings, your intuition, and the flow of energy. This section focuses on the Soulcation principles of energy management, and offers tools and tactics for how to create space in your daily calendar, physical home, and inner world so you have the bandwidth to make the necessary shifts to the Soulcation lifestyle.

Finally, in Part III ("How to Design a Life You Don't Need A Vacation From") we get very practical with the 7-step Soulcation Framework (which I call "FUN-work"). This framework applies the principles of design-thinking, vacation blueprints, and emotional healing to form the basis of how you shift to a Soulcation lifestyle. It will teach you how to study who you are on vacation, make a Happy List, leverage the "HELL NO / FUCK YES" filter to stay in alignment with your energy, and map out a new lifestyle you can integrate into your everyday life.

In the pages of this book, you will have a chance to go back to who you were as an uninhibited child and explore what you would want to do if you ignored other people's expectations, opinions, and even advice. Once you have this clarity, you can start your own Soulcation by incorporating new vacation-y habits into your everyday life. You become your own master permission-giver: tuning into your energy (more than your calendar), designing happy experiments, and letting your external actions ebb and flow based on your internal emotional weather. Through learning the life-design skills of Soulcation, you will never abandon yourself, your desires, your needs, or your wants for the sake of someone or something else. You will be clear on how you want to feel, and you make decisions in pursuit of these feelings goals before any other achievement goals.

THE PATH YOU HAVEN'T TRIED

This book is a simplified manual of everything I found and learned in my own pursuit of a Soulcation lifestyle. I've compiled it here around a singular concept—that the cure to our generation's burnout epidemic is to tear down our busy calendars and incorporate more rest, play, and pleasure into everyday living. I've kept the practices simple, as I know when the body is full of stress and anxiety, reaching for new tools is difficult. You need options that feel easy, manageable, and that have a high likelihood of giving you the relief you seek.

I started this introduction with the lie that working harder will make us happy. The truth is, it's possible to reach one version of success, while still experiencing burnout, anxiety, depression, and a general malaise about life. The only definition of success worthy of your time and effort is one where your head hits the pillow each night and you think to yourself, "Heck yes, my soul felt fully alive today." If you don't feel quite there yet, rest assured, there is another way to live. I've written this book and launched all the accompanying resources at takeasoulcation.com (including a workbook, course, and mentorship offerings) in order for you to live that way.

Sister, I know you're tired. But you are in need of a different kind of vacation and a different type of break. It's time to start your Soulcation.

PART I:

BURNOUT

CHAPTER 1: IT ALL FALLS APART

I blinked hard, trying to stop the image of a naked African girl from whipping across my mind. My palms were sweating, my head reeled, and my breakfast was not sitting well. I tried to watch the slides being presented, but that image, the face of that dehydrated, famished child sitting in a blue bucket wouldn't leave the forefront of my mind. It had hung on the wall since the very first day Bill and Melinda Gates opened this office, intended to remind staff of the faces behind the staggering global numbers: Half a million children die each year from malaria.

That day, it felt like I was the girl in the blue bucket. My heart was pounding, my throat was constricting, and my body was heating to an unusual boil for a dark winter day. My water bottle set where it always did at my feet, but I couldn't even muster the energy to reach down. An open notebook was on the table in front of me, my usual column of hand-drawn boxes running down the left of the page, which I would check off with great satisfaction as I moved through my to-do list.

I'd been working in this iconic office building across from Seattle's Space Needle, for nearly five years. In many ways it was more familiar to me than my own home, which I rarely saw in the daylight anymore. The floor to ceiling glass, perpetually stocked Starbucks coffee, hallways adorned with African art, and this lake-view conference room, where everything from the whiteboard walls to the secret drawer with the extra computer chargers made it feel like somewhere I belonged. I knew where to sit to watch the seaplanes land in Lake Union or to avoid having to be the one managing the pesky international conferencing system.

But today I felt my underarms sweating, and wiped my brow self-consciously, hunching over enough in my chair to keep the vomit at bay. I hoped no one noticed anything. Earlier, I had walked down Fifth Avenue looking the same as I always did: a navy suit dress from my all-navy wardrobe and a string of pearls from my grandmother.

Could this be the start of a cold? Maybe it's leftover jet lag from last week's trip to Zambia?

I'd stayed up late the night before in a terrible fight with my husband, but what I felt wasn't overtired. My body trembled, and the photo of the girl was pixelating. I started pinching myself in hopes it was all a nightmare.

My inner voice was screaming, *Danger, danger, danger ... get out of here!* even as I heard my boss, Diana, ask from across the room, "Mel, what do you think about this investment?" I stared blankly past her face, convinced I was being transported back to the heat, blue bucket, and despair of the African village.

"Um, one second," I said, pushing myself away from the table to make a beeline for the bathroom.

I hurled through the heavy door and made no effort to shut it behind me, as I collapsed on the white tile floor. I struggled to breathe, my body curled into a fetal position, and I moved only enough to aim into the toilet to vomit every few minutes. A dizzy, spinning feeling zipped through me like electricity, seeping into every corner of my body and filling me with pain.

I looked down at my watch to see how much time had passed, hoping whatever nightmare I was living would pass quickly. The rest of my team was still in the lake-view conference room, and I suspected I only had a few more minutes before Diana came to check on me. *What do I say to her?* I was used to being the girl who had my shit together.

Maybe I have cancer? I considered the idea that something bad—like, really bad—was about to turn my life upside down. I imagined myself in a blue hospital gown attached to IV lines, fighting for my life. The irony of the next idea shocked me. *Maybe life in the hospital will actually feel like a break ... a vacation from emails, chores, and taking care of all the things for all the people. In hospitals people get to rest, and gosh, do I need some rest.*

I could picture it: just me and an IV pumping magic happy juice in my veins. No visitors or distractions, and definitely no laptop. I'd finally get time to myself, to think about ME for once. It actually sounded like a nice escape, assuming I could find a way to move from my position with my head hanging over the automatic flush toilet in the cold Gates Foundation office bathroom.

THE INVISIBLE PAIN: LIVING "GOOD ENOUGH"

If your life looks anything like mine did a few years ago, you're on a mission. You know how to check the boxes, chase success, and exceed expectations. Maybe you've experienced some mistakes along the way, but they've served as meaningful life lessons. You've likely hit some milestones and are on your way to the life you always thought you wanted. Perhaps the story in your head for how life should go is playing out—definitely not perfectly—but pages are turning, life is happening, and a steady flow of wind is behind your back, propelling you forward. You've laid the foundation, painted the walls, and decorated the metaphorical home that is your life.

You've made peace with the decisions you made in years past and a large amount of your time and energy feels spoken for. There is so much to be grateful for—and in some ways, that makes you feel guilty for feeling so tired, anxious, and yes, sometimes depressed, in a life that looks so shiny on the outside. *Who am I to want more when I have so much*? you think.

Maybe, like me, under the hood, your day-to-day involves juggling a shitload of tasks. My calendar felt like a Tetris game I could never win. I would wake up and check my email before even getting out of bed, then move to mentally drafting responses while I blow-dried my hair. Somewhere deep down, I knew the energy I expended in service of others, my job, and my family was leaving me depleted. The caffeine pills I took in secret, the chronic gut illnesses my doctors couldn't seem to get to the bottom of, and the routine of crashing into my bed at night without even washing my face, didn't seem like the version of "success" I had spent so many years chasing. I felt pulled in a million directions, squeezing out every productive ounce of energy I could muster, only to earn myself a night of takeout, wine, and binge-watching Netflix on Friday night.

Still, Monday would come along, and I'd head to the Gates Foundation and spend hours in meetings stress-biting my nails under the table and leaving a tiny trail of dead flesh for the janitorial staff to vacuum each night. During breaks between meetings, I would head to the bathroom and pick my acne-prone skin, frustrated with all the adult pimples that reminded me of the stress I couldn't seem to escape. By afternoon, you'd find me in the kitchen with a third cup of coffee and handful of Reese's Pieces, using sugar and caffeine as company-approved drugs to help me "get through the day." As I bounced from work meetings to my desk, I kept a list of the tasks

I would need to do that evening, convinced that a successful life required being highly productive well past dinner time.

I remember the day Diana popped into our work kitchen and said, "How you are holding up, Mel?"

"I'm *fine*, thanks for asking," I responded. "And you?"

"Yup, *fine* too," she responded, with a half-fake smile.

Fine was a secret code word. Something I learned from my mother, who learned it from her mother. A good girl's form of bullshitting her way through a bad day. If I was really honest with myself, I used "fine" to tolerate the fatigue brought on by busy, and to convince myself I was strong enough to push through it anyway. By telling myself I was fine, I could stuff the pain deep enough down into an internal dungeon, where it wouldn't really exist, or at least wasn't *really* that bad. This tactic helped me live "just fine" for years. Fine was manageable, doable, tolerable, and honestly, the only version of life I really knew. Fine was familiar, and I'd rather swim in the pool of familiar pain than test the waters of a pain that (heaven forbid) was worse than fine. In fact, fine was my surface-level response to not just Diana, but to friends, family members, and far too frequently, my husband, when I sure didn't want to wade through the confusing, emotional messiness simmering under the surface of my seemingly fine life.

DOCTOR, I'M FINE

Despite being a global health professional who should have known better, *fine* was even my default with my doctor. A year before I collapsed on the white tile of the Gates Foundation bathroom floor, I had to pick up some malaria medicine for an upcoming international trip.

"Welcome, Mel, good to see you today," my doctor said. "I see you're here for travel medicine. I'm happy to help. Please sit down." I sat.

She had questions. "Can I ask you, how are you holding up with all the work travel? It's been a lot this year." She looked at me with compassionate, concerned eyes.

"Fine, managing just fine."

Something in her eyes vibrated down my spine, as I nervously contemplated her calling my bluff.

She continued, "You look fatigued. Just to be extra cautious, I'm going to take your blood pressure and heart rate."

Oh no, please don't, I thought.

That's when she found my secret. My heart rate was off the charts. I couldn't *fine* my way out of the one hundred beats per minutes she just counted. It was a Monday. A normal workday. And my heart was ticking like a seventy-year-old man with heart disease.

"Mel, it appears your heart is under stress. Typically, when I see this in such young, healthy patients it's because of emotional stress. I'm not letting you leave here until you take some deep breaths, and we get the heart rate down," she said gently, but firmly.

She laid me down on her cozy couch and poured me a cup of tea, while I regretted the fact that out of all the doctors in town, I had chosen a holistic medicine doctor. "I know it sounds crazy coming from a doctor, but talking about feelings can really help the body," she said.

"Talking about your feelings has shown to have a positive effect on regulating the nervous system and reducing anxiety," she went on with a clinical tone. "You're living under a lot of stress at work. Talking with someone might help."

She wrote me a referral to a psychiatrist, with the word "anxiety" on the diagnosis line.

No way, I can't have anxiety.

I had read enough about anxiety to understand why some people collapse under its weight in seasons of suffering, but in every area of my life there was evidence I was staying afloat.

I'm a successful adult with a good job, good house, and a good life, thank you very much. I take my daily vitamins and heck, even get most of my servings of vegetables in. Just give me my travel medicine and send me on my way.

Yet walking away from the appointment, I couldn't deny there was a heaviness in my heart. Some days a panicky heaviness. I longed for relief.

Maybe I just need a vacation? That always does the trick, I thought.

But as I walked back through my office doors, I had this weird feeling of gratitude for the busyness of my life. I belonged here—juggling, hustling, working my ass off. Even more, I was needed here, and being needed felt good. The life I created around being a busy public servant, wife, and friend always willing to say "yes" was the only thing I really knew. I felt at home in the busy chaos of always being on. It made me feel important, purposeful, successful. For years, I had been fighting with all my heart to advance the Bill & Melinda Gates Foundation's vision of malaria eradication. Africa was my battleground, colleagues were my combat brigade, and our plan was to fight like hell on behalf of children dying from malaria. And while sure, sometimes it made my heart beat one hundred times a minute, I justified all my busyness as being "the good kind of busy."

Yet somehow amidst this purpose-driven fight, the oxygen was seeping out of me. I had always chosen working towards future success over present rest—and it was catching up to me.

As I opened my computer, I couldn't help but wonder...

Maybe the doctor was right. Was something more at play here?

Could this not just be about fighting *against* malaria but fighting *for* my own life? In my effort to be in service of others, could it be possible I forgot about the most important fight of all—the fight for my own joy and happiness?

YOU CAN ALWAYS CHANGE YOUR LIFE

Fast forward. It had been a year since I'd last been awed by the glimmering glass of the Bill & Melinda Gates Foundation building. Instead of my navy capsule wardrobe, I was wearing a bright green dress with roaming orange tigers, a symbol of the wild and free Mel emerging on the other side of one of the most radical decisions of my life. My armpits were sweating, this time for a good reason. It felt like my awkward college reunion all over again, except I would be wading into the sea of work colleagues, where topics such as anxiety, panic attacks, burnout, death, divorce, or sabbaticals were not the norm.

What do I tell them? I wondered.

How do I NOT come across as an arrogant, privileged snob for talking about how I sold all my belongings and spent the down payment I had saved for my first house on traveling the world for a year? Do I admit I've designed an even better life than what I had when I was here, in this world?

I was aware my life updates all involved giving a grand middle finger to the typical script people roll into midlife with. The fear of being misunderstood, or worse, judged, had me in a bathroom stall trying to dry my armpits with toilet paper even before the party started.

It was the day of the Gates Foundation's annual Fourth of July picnic. The company event takes over a large portion of Seattle Center, the iconic public space that houses the Space Needle, where themed food stalls, live music, and endless free booze gives everyone a reason to ditch work early. There are even cartoon characters walking around to entertain the kids, while parents huddle together and secretly (or not so secretly) keep talking about work.

"Mel!" I heard from a dark-haired woman in a simple T-shirt and jeans. It was Meg, the Foundation's malaria advocacy lead and one of my favorite colleagues. Her smile was inviting and electric—like something I would receive from my own mother. "Come here," she said, wrapping me in a full hug and holding me a bit longer than normal, while she most definitely got a whiff of the sweat oozing out of my arms.

"How are you, Mel?" she says. "I love that dress. You look so good." Then she pulled back and looked closely at me, scanning my eyes. My face was sun-kissed, finally clear of all the stress acne and layers of caked-on makeup I used to wear to hide it. I finally didn't need to hide the dark jet-lag circles or the late nights fighting with my husband.

"I've been following your journey on Instagram," Meg mentioned. "It looks like you have had THE TIME OF YOUR LIFE!"

My stomach tightened. When I left my Seattle life in a hurried panic, I was too afraid to tell people the full truth. *Heck, most days I was afraid to even admit it to myself.* Meg knew the Mel with the good-girl masks, people-pleasing armor, and unrelenting fire to be productive, no matter what the cost. She'd been my senior, and I sure as heck had cared what she thought. When I said goodbye to her the year prior, she had no idea all the dark shadows haunting me under the surface. But in the months following, when I was cracking open but still afraid to admit them out loud, I started writing them on Instagram. That's when it hit me: *Holy shit—she knows.*

My Instagram posts had been honest and raw, with long captions of me processing all the pain I had kept buried away for no one to see most of my life. Sure, there were filtered photos of me drinking wine in Paris, frolicking on the beach in Thailand, and floating in the Dead Sea in Israel, but underneath them sat a woman going through her "dark night of the soul." Being so far away somehow gave me courage to say out loud the big, scary things that for years I had kept silent.

"Mel, we miss you. Gosh, the team sure wishes you were around. How ARE YOU?"

"I'm good, Meg, really good," I responded. "It has been the best year of my life—fun and wild and unexpected in every way. I went through hell and made it to the other side."

"Mel, you're such an inspiration, you know that, right?! I've always wondered what life might be like outside the grind. I wish I was brave enough to do something like you did."

Brave. I had only thought of myself as desperate and at the end of myself, not brave. It's only the emotional wrecks who raise the white flag and call it quits on everything they once knew, isn't it?

“It’s crazy,” I said. “The whole ‘leap and the net shall appear’ thing is true. I’m happy, Meg. Really happy. And it’s blowing my mind there is this much joy on the other side.”

“Time for a celebratory drink,” she winked.

As we walked over to the outdoor bar decked out like a Monopoly game board with kids running around, I was reminded of all the moms juggling their jobs, work, and caring for these kiddos at home. *When will they get time for THEMSELVES today*? I wondered. *How can any woman claim time for herself in a world constantly screaming for her attention and service?*

For a moment, I scanned all the familiar faces I used to be intimidated by and remembered all the mental gymnastics I went through to climb my way up the ladder. Perhaps their stories were slightly different than mine, but the gap between us felt thinner. Perhaps the fact that I once felt busy and worn down and in desperate need of a break was because that was, in fact, exactly what I needed. Maybe it’s exactly what we all need sometimes. I just wished it hadn’t taken me hitting rock bottom before I woke up and realized it.

CHAPTER 2: BURNOUT

It was six months after that day on the Gates Foundation bathroom floor.

I woke up to a tall, attractive doctor shaking me out of a deep sleep. I blinked my eyes a few times to see his face right above mine. I looked down at the IV line dripping into my arm and the tangled hospital gown draped around my body. Last thing I remembered, I had been curled up in a fetal position around the toilet after profuse vomiting, the culmination of another ugly fight with my husband.

Is this all a nightmare? And am I really at the hospital? Oh no, we have dinner plans tonight, and I still haven't baked the dessert.

The doctor sat down on a stool, scooting close to my bed and taking a couple of seconds to settle himself. Gently touching my hand, I felt a spark of electricity shoot through me. I hadn't been touched with such kindness in months. The caring aspect of his eyes and the tingling sensation were both unfamiliar and enticing.

"I have good news and bad news," he said. "The good news is all your labs came back clear. No brain aneurysm or signs of seizure. Nothing showed up on your bloodwork either. Everything looks good."

That's it? Is that the good news or the bad news? I was starting to remember how my husband brought me into this emergency room the night before after hours of sweating, dizziness, and uncontrollable vomiting.

"The bad news is ... it seems as if you were having a panic attack. In the medical world we call it panic attack anxiety, the most severe form of anxiety."

Panic attack? Impossible.

I couldn't leave the hospital and tell my family this was the diagnosis. I was going to need a second opinion. Hot Doctor must have missed something. Here I was in one of the best hospitals in the state, with symptoms I swear were signs of me dying, and this was all they had for me? A diagnosis of panic felt like a slap in the face—the epitome of shame for a strong, reliable, high-achieving woman. *The Mels of this world don't end up in an emergency room just because of anxiety.*

For my entire life I'd prided myself on "managing" my emotions: locking up the painful ones I didn't want to feel in some unused compartment in my brain, turning off the lights, and moving on. I'd come to believe this was a skill anyone could acquire, and one I used liberally. I surveyed the areas of my life—work, home, family, finances, etc.—and concluded nothing was really wrong. But why would my body be sending me a different message? My emotional override function was no longer working. The part of my brain that stored all the pain and trauma I avoided thinking about had failed. Like any failed operating system, it needed to be reset—and fast.

"Mel, a panic attack is simply an intense physical manifestation of anxiety," Hot Doctor said. "They're very common, actually. One of the most common disorders among women in the United States, in fact. Sometimes when we're faced with heightened stress, in order to protect us, our body stops us in our tracks." He went on to explain panic attacks involve an unexpected but brief burst of fear accompanied by physical "fight or flight" symptoms such as nausea, a racing heart, hot flashes, shortness of breath, or chest pain. "What most people don't know is the nervous system can't always tell the difference between physical pain and emotional pain," he went on. "And when we are carrying unprocessed emotional pain, our nervous system can react to make us sick. This is just your body acting as your internal doctor of sorts," he said with a wink and brushed his hand on my shoulder.

"Most people experience this in their own home and never get help. Consider yourself a lucky one," he said, sounding like this whole situation was a good thing. "I'll keep you on this IV for another few hours. We've added some pain medicine that will help calm the nerves. But tell me, are there any stressors in your life that you think might have caused this?"

"No, Doctor, no, I can't think of any," I said immediately, before even thinking.

He held my gaze while we both sat with the awkward silence. He was going to wait for me to start. "Well, things at work have been a bit busy. I've been away from home quite a bit, and the jet lag sometimes gets to me," I said.

He stayed seated on his doctor stool, silent. "I don't get to spend enough time with my husband, so that makes things hard. We seem to always be busy—crossing paths, you know." More silence. "And my mom is ill. I've been spending lots of days taking care of her while she's been in the hospital." Silence, again.

"It sounds like you're experiencing a case of burnout," he said. "And I'm pleased to report burnout has been shown to be completely reversable with rest and therapy."

BURNOUT AND THE EMOTIONAL EXHAUSTION EPIDEMIC

One in four women have experienced clinical anxiety in the past year, which includes worried thoughts, a feeling of unease, and emotional exhaustion.[1] This anxiety, experienced over a sustained period of days, weeks, and years in the human nervous system, will inevitably lead to burnout. According to Buzzfeed writer and author Anne Helen Petersen, "Burnout is when you hit the wall—but instead of collapsing, or taking a rest, you scale the wall, and just keep going."[2]

Sound familiar? She goes on to say, "Burnout arrives when every corner of our life feels unstable, and we convince ourselves that working all the time is what will fix it."

This art of "convincing ourselves that working more will fix it" is what I believe is behind what we far too often label as "stress," and arguably why burnout is both so stealthy and prevalent.

Evidence shows we are the most stressed-out generation of women in human history. Pre-COVID-19 pandemic, according to a CNBC and SurveyMonkey poll, self-reported rates of stress and burnout were sixty-eight percent among women.[3] Twenty to thirty percent of teachers have moderately high to high levels of burnout. Similar rates are found in studies among professors, medical doctors, and international aid workers. As a clinical diagnosis, burnout is most often used to describe the physical or mental collapse as the result of overwork in a job or career. However, when researcher Herbert Freudenberger first coined the term in 1975, "burnout" was defined by three components:

1. *emotional exhaustion*—the fatigue that comes from caring too much, for too long;
2. *depersonalization*—the depletion of empathy, caring, and compassion; and
3. *decreased sense of accomplishment*—an unconquerable sense of futility; feeling that nothing you do makes any difference.

In their book *Burnout: The Secret to Unlocking the Stress Cycle*, Emily Nagoski and Amelia Nagoski report that after decades of additional research, it's the first element in burnout, *emotional exhaustion*, most strongly linked to negative impacts on our health, relationships, and work.[4] *Emotional exhaustion* is arguably the silent pandemic of our generation. This is especially the case for women, who are conducting hours of invisible labor outside the traditional workplace: a type of work often associated with emotional exhaustion.

If exhaustion is going to the point where you can't physically go any further, *emotional exhaustion* is carrying emotions—both yours and others'—to the point where you feel like you can't carry them any further. To be female and express your femininity inherently involves emotional labor, including tending to others' emotions. It's a superpower we have been endowed with by the universe, and something I believe should be celebrated, adored, and even compensated. Yet when left unrestrained, this emotional labor becomes the very thing that keeps us burned out and sick. It's a superpower that arguably, over centuries, society has taken advantage of, abused, and then normalized in the form of emotional exhaustion. Women label it as "stress," "overwhelm," "tiredness," or maybe if things get really bad, a "midlife crisis." We say to ourselves, "It's normal, keep going, you can do hard things," yet deep down our soul is tired of tending to everyone else's emotions except our own. The undercurrent of unprocessed emotions is stored in our bodies and is screaming for relief.

We all know that sensation of something rumbling inside of us: that hum that keeps us on edge, grasping for something about our lives to be different. But if we want to reverse emotional exhaustion, first we must understand what emotions are, how they show up inside us, and most importantly, how we exhaust them. According to Emily and Amelia Nagoski:

> *Emotions, at their most basic level, involve the release of neurochemicals in the brain in response to some stimulus. You see the person you have a crush on across the room, your brain releases a bunch of chemicals, and that triggers a cascade of physiological changes—your heart beats faster, your hormones shift, and your stomach flutters. You take a deep breath and sigh. Your facial expression changes; maybe you blush; even the timbre of your voice becomes warmer. Your thoughts shift to memories of the crush and fantasies about the future, and you suddenly feel an urge to cross the room and say hi. Just about every system in your body responds to the chemical and electrical cascade activated by the sight of the person.*
>
> *That's emotion. It's automatic and instantaneous. It happens everywhere, and it affects everything. And it's happening all the time—we feel many different emotions simultaneously, even in response to one stimulus. You may feel an urge to approach your crush, but also, simultaneously, feel an urge to turn away and pretend you didn't notice them.*
>
> *Left to their own devices, emotions—these instantaneous, whole-body reactions to some stimulus—will end on their own. Your attention shifts from your crush to some other topic, and the flush of infatuation eases, until that certain special someone crosses your mind or your path once*

more. The same goes for the jolt of pain you feel when someone is cruel to you or the flash of disgust when you smell something unpleasant. They just end.

In short, emotions are tunnels. If you go all the way through them, you get to the light at the end. Exhaustion happens when we get stuck in an emotion.

When we don't create space in life to travel through the tunnel of each emotion, however long that tunnel might be, they get stuck. And stuck emotions are at the root of burnout. Their "stuck-ness" can often show up in panic attacks (like it did for me) as well as migraines, digestive problems, short-windedness, rashes, chronic pain, autoimmune diseases, or a host of other illness. The body doesn't lie—your emotional exhaustion needs to move somewhere. If there is no space in your life to process uncomfortable emotions, no wonder anxiety, emotional overwhelm, and burnout ensue.

WHY IT'S HARD TO SLOW DOWN

If traveling through the tunnel of an emotion is what we need to reverse emotional exhaustion, slowing down to a safe enough speed to enter the tunnel is an essential first step. If you've ever driven through a mountain pass with a one-lane tunnel, you know you can't speed through it at sixty miles an hour without risking a crash. Slowing down is key to emotional well-being, and yet the question I get asked most often by women is, "Why is slowing down so hard, and how do I do it?"

Hundreds of wellness magazines write articles on this question each month, but Soulcation is grounded in the belief the root problem has a hell of a lot to do with internalized capitalism. Dr. Emilia Roig said, "Capitalism is to us like water is to fish. We do not notice that it surrounds us."[5]

I would argue capitalism has infiltrated modern society so deeply this same fish-water situation now applies to internalized capitalism, which is the state in which one equates their productivity, achievements, or accomplishments with their self-worth.

Capitalism has been around for a couple hundred years, running our economies and our governments, and perhaps what we haven't realized, collectively influencing our internal beliefs about ourselves as well. Essentially, internalized capitalism keeps us obsessed with productivity. We spend far more time in a *doing* state than a *being* state. Unconsciously, we've bought into the belief our value comes from doing, and have dedicated a majority of our energy to productivity. Skeptical you are influenced by internalized capitalism? Here are the signs it's impacting your life:

1. **You feel guilty for resting.** You don't let yourself rest, even after long days, tiring experiences, or triggering emotions. You deny yourself what your body legitimately needs out of guilt or worry that it will cost you productivity. Your internal dialogue around rest is often: "I want to rest, but I'm already falling behind." Ultimately, rest never feels as good as it could because you feel guilty when you're doing it.
2. **You place productivity before your health.** Health is arguably a long-term game, a series of daily right actions (good sleep, nutritious food, strong connections) that add up to physical and mental well-being over a lifetime. But

internalized capitalism keeps us focused on the seemingly "urgent" needs at hand. Because internalized capitalism is a belief system that taps into our survival instincts, it compels us to pull that all-nighter, help someone else before helping ourselves, or complete everything on our to-do list before taking care of our health. Productivity is made out to be urgent and essential. Health and well-being are deprioritized as "nice to have."

3. **You believe that hard work equals happiness.** In internalized capitalism, when you don't feel satisfied or happy in life, you believe the best way forward is to work harder. You think happiness will come with the next house or promotion, or upon completion of an intense season. You subconsciously accept happiness is something only afforded to people who work hard and endure (rather than a birthright).
4. **You feel lazy, even when you're experiencing pain, trauma, or adversity.** I hear this one all too often with clients. They come to me usually in significant life moments—a job change, the end of a relationship, or some crisis that has brought them to the end of themselves. These are the seasons in life when going slow, extreme self-compassion, and giving yourself permission to do not much of anything are so important. But I find it's also when the monkey mind of internalized capitalism kicks in and tells us, "You should be back at work" or "You should be doing more." We see rest as laziness, rather than as the necessary remedy for moving through life's inevitable emotional tunnels of grief and pain.
5. **You use busyness to avoid your needs**. Internalized capitalism is based on the belief your needs are less import-

ant than what you accomplish. This belief can lead you to deny, suppress, ignore, or dismiss basic needs such as sleep, rest, love, or care from another, for the sake of "honoring a commitment" or marching forward with a plan to accomplish something. We also use "staying busy" as a coping strategy. It's easier to maintain a full calendar, a long to-do list, and a full set of social and professional engagements than it is to get still, listen, and travel through the emotional tunnels of your life.

6. **Your self-worth is largely based on doing well in your career.** Since the time you were young, you have crafted an understanding of your identity around work. You put a lot of energy and effort into planning the next steps in your career, and working towards more pay, a better title, and a validating performance review. Your sense of safety and importance is connected to how things are going at work.

As you can see, internalized capitalism offers a version of "success" for life that many of us, to some extent, have probably unconsciously bought into. When success is associated with busying yourself with action after action, at the expense of meeting your core physical and emotional needs, it's no wonder you find yourself exhausted and never make it through the emotional tunnel.

THE ART OF CREATING SPACE

The hospital room taught me an important lesson. I needed a different type of medicine and a different type of break. The ER brought me to an abrupt halt. It also catalyzed a radically different approach from the "working more will fix it" mentality I had unconsciously been running on repeat for my entire life.

My panic attack forced me to face the very thing I had been hiding from the world—and even worse, from myself: I was unconsciously living asleep. I was repressing the emotions that were too overwhelming, but also asleep to my needs, desires, freedom, and big, wild dreams. My busyness kept me numb and staved off me noticing the emotional exhaustion, but it wasn't a cure. The "good girl" programming I inherited as a child was still running, and in order to really change, I would need to dismantle it.

If you remember one thing from *Soulcation*, may it be that you need to *learn how to unlearn* to create the change you want. Too many self-help gurus sell you on learning, offering more courses, books, and curriculum, as if filling up your intellectual tank will resolve your emotional exhaustion. As a person who has both researched and recovered from emotional exhaustion, I'm convinced answers will not come through fighting back against the pain, and definitely not through us learning the latest, trendy life hack. The key ingredient to real, lasting change is unlearning.

I'll explain more about the art and science of unlearning in future chapters—but I'm here now to say it will save your life. Ultimately, for those of us emotionally exhausted, anxious, and burned out, I am convinced it is rest, play, and pleasure that will heal us. We must slow down, do less, and create a lot of blank space before we can birth a new Soulcation-style life. We must be willing to let things crumble, die, and lay dormant. We must unlearn all the actions and beliefs that keep us in the vicious cycle of over-extending, reaching emotional exhaustion, and ignoring it and pushing through anyway. This is because the cold, hard truth is that it's not action you have trouble with, but inaction. And inaction and doing nothing is exactly what will save our generation from collective burnout.

Welcome to Soulcation—the concept of expansive, spacious time for slowing down, resting, and traveling through the tunnels of each emotion. It's not about pulling out a credit card and booking a room at a resort, and it doesn't require an airplane ticket or a Pinterest-worthy A-frame cabin in the mountains. A Soulcation is all about tuning down the noise of the world so you can hear the quiet whisper of your own soul, and then cultivating the skills to tend to and feel all the emotions that come up.

I will walk you through the process of taking a Soulcation to heal your emotional exhaustion and avoid burnout. First, we'll cover strategies that don't work and the remedies we try that actually keep us living on autopilot. Second, we will dive into practical ways to give your soul exactly what you need without compromising other priorities. Then, I'll teach you the principles and steps of a Soulcation. And, finally, you'll learn how to redesign your daily life so that it feels good.

But be prepared: Taking a Soulcation is not adding a set of routines to your calendar. You're already a rock star at that—and my guess is you wouldn't have picked up this book if you wanted to add more things to your list. The secret sauce of life change is leveraging play, rest, and pleasure as the gateways to your soul's greatest transformation. It's the path too often we fail to try, but I believe it's the only path to full freedom. We must start living softer, sisters, not harder. Our lives literally depend on it. And I've written this book to show you how. My own Soulcation serves as the backbone for all my recommendations. I share how I went from living as a clinically anxious, burned-out Gates Foundation staffer and professional people-pleaser to a blossoming creative who runs a business from the beach, lives life as my own boss, and never feels guilty for giving myself the naps, dance breaks, and orgasms I need. I'm not here to sugarcoat this and tell you it's easy. You have likely tried lots of other paths with only modest results at best. The bad news is Soulcation involves slowing down, doing less, and embracing the principals of essentialism and minimalism for your soul, which goes against Western cultural norms and expectations. The good news is Soulcation uses rest, play, and pleasure, the very things that feel good, as the gateways to access your inner knowing, trust your intuition, heal your pain, and change your life. The result? You can be truly free.

So, if you're ready to finally make space to give yourself what *you* need, and declare your soul your top priority, read on.

CHAPTER 3: THE LIE THAT "EVERYTHING IS BETTER ON VACATION"

What I really need is a vacation.

This thought ran through my mind on repeat for years. I would push myself to the brink during the workweek—skipping meals, not exercising, and living off too much coffee—only to crash each weekend, binge-watching Netflix and falling asleep on the couch without the energy to walk to bed. Rest was getting eight hours of sleep once a week. And my annual two-week beach vacation was the breadcrumb for which I held out hope. *Everything will be better once I'm on vacation.* Or so I thought.

MY OWN ESCAPE

A year into my new marriage, the same year I had the devastating panic attack, my mom was diagnosed with a rare, aggressive type of bone cancer. She was fifty-three, and doctors told us they would need to amputate her leg to try to save her. The surgery was high-risk, and there were no guarantees of removing all the cancer.

Within weeks of the diagnosis, my dad, brother, and I were taking shifts at the hospital. I worked from her bedside (using the windowless bereavement room to take virtual meetings), kept her room supplied with Trader Joe's snacks (because I believe in a world where no one should have to live off only hospital food), updated extended family on the leg-chopping developments, and coordinated the flow of humans who wanted to visit my new, but arguably not improved, one-legged mom. I imagine I also paid my bills and washed my sheets at some point, but I really don't remember. My husband, an artist in a new band at the time, popped in when he could. He would run an errand or bring by takeout when I asked, but his absence at the hospital became a point of constant fighting.

One night when the hospital was quiet, Mom was watching *West Wing,* and I was on my laptop, working as usual. She reached over and put her hand on my arm. I looked up surprised, as this touch was out of character for my mother, who didn't often express deep emotions. "Mel, you need to be taking care of yourself," she said, in a way only a mother can do. "It's 11:00 p.m., and you're still working away. Rest, honey. This is going to be a long road."

Ha, take care of myself. Has she forgotten the doctors are running out of options and we're playing a high-stakes game of survival right now? What does she want me to do, go to the freaking spa?

Ironically, I learned my non-resting ways from her. All my life, she was helpful, resourceful, and a busy bee with no low gear. She volunteered at our church, served on boards, and cooked daily hot meals for the family. I couldn't remember Mom taking herself to the spa or checking out of our lives to take care of herself. Perhaps she did this in secret, but despite all the good things this woman taught me, rest was not one of them. I never saw her putting herself first. *How dare she suggest I start doing that now!*

I resisted the idea of letting go of any of my responsibilities for weeks, both out of the absurdness of me leaving her at this moment, and also because I didn't know what the hell I would actually do to "rest." Rest was not a subject I ever took in school (*I wish!*). But finally, when my mom started to set an alarm for 10:00 p.m. each night to remind me to leave the hospital, I started to accept my days of work and caretaking allowed no time for rest, or for ME. I booked two nights at a Holiday Inn, packed the cleanest pair of sweatpants I could find, and drove out of town with the nebulous goal of clearing my head and refilling my tank with just enough mojo to avoid a full implosion. Driving into the quaint oceanfront town of Bellingham, Washington, I could see Main Street's local ice cream shop, boutiques, and seafront boardwalk from the lobby. Yet when I walked in my hotel room, I collapsed on the bed. It was one o'clock in the afternoon, but all I wanted to do was lay supine—no people, no email, and no noise.

Next thing I knew, it was dark. I woke the next morning to the TV remote under my arm, and after some bitter hotel room coffee, pushed play again, binge-watching yet another season of *Madam Secretary*. When I was at the hospital busy with tasks, I could stay somewhat positive. But here, all alone, my mind latched onto what I feared the most. *She's not going to make it. She's going to die,* I kept thinking to myself, as I buried my head in the pillow to cry ugly, breathless tears. I would try to recall the blur of the last few months, but mostly the only memory I had was of me holding myself together all day, only to burst into tears the second I shut my car door and was alone for the late-night drive home. The car was my sanctuary; not even my husband knew how many tears I cried alone there before I mustered up the strength to come in the house. This "rest and recharge" weekend felt like an extended version of these car rides. My tears kept coming and coming, and their intensity scared me. I was paralyzed in bed, unable to move from the weight of the sadness. *Would this pain ever end?* Deep in my bones I wasn't sure.

Yes, my mom was dying. But it wasn't just that. Under the surface, I didn't want to admit to myself the other, deeper truths. In the wake of my mom's illness, my new husband, Brock, was surprisingly absent. Struggling with his own depression, he was unable to meet me in my own grief and sadness, and it was putting our marriage in dire straits. I felt hurt, unseen, and disconnected from him, the person who I had vowed to be with "in sickness and in health." Our home life was in disarray—our lease was ending and we couldn't agree on what to do next, Brock was traveling lots for the band, and I forgot to pay a parking ticket and now owed a sizeable amount of money to get it off my record. I had dozens of unanswered work emails, and had fallen in the habit of opening emails, then closing them—unable to muster the energy to do my job. I couldn't remember the last time I exercised. I ate whatever I could find. I even bought new underwear off Amazon when laundry felt too hard. I kept the facade of life going on the outside, but inside, I was anxious, disappointed, and *emotionally lonely*.

This stuffed-down inner reality rose to the surface in the silence of that hotel weekend. Feeling all of it sent me into a forty-eight-hour paralysis. It felt like I had just jumped off Ireland's Cliffs of Moher without ever being taught how to fucking swim. Returning to my hyper-busy life in Seattle was the only flotation device I knew of to save myself. Busyness distracted me from the *emotional exhaustion* I didn't want—let alone know how—to face. I left the Holiday Inn earlier than intended that weekend, telling myself I had too much to do to keep lying in bed.

WE ARE IN DESPERATE NEED OF A *DIFFERENT KIND OF REST*

Sarah is a client of mine. She is a talented and ambitious mid-thirty-something who works at Microsoft. When she first began coaching with me, we did a detailed survey of the rhythms of rest she was *currently* engaging in. I forced her to comb through her online and paper calendars, family schedules, and past vacations, and I asked pointed questions about how she *really* spent her time. What we found is that Sarah, a successful and busy working woman, had far more time for rest than she thought. Her perception of her time compared to her reality was skewed. The problem for Sarah, and for millions of women like her, is that rest is too often unintentional, unplanned, and occurs below the surface of conscious enjoyment. Sarah's story begs the question:

Why do we always underestimate the amount of time we have for rest?

And if women are resting more than we think, why do we find ourselves in the most emoitonally exhasuted and over-extended generation of human history?

As I explained to Sarah, it's because of what I call the *fake rest effect*. Most women are masters of this skill. In order to stay alive, Sarah's body needs some form of rest on a daily basis. (I'll explain the problem with the most common form of rest in a moment). Although she doesn't realize it, Sarah is a *fake rester*. She pushes herself to the brink. She may end the day on the couch, scrolling her phone or watching TV. Or maybe the TV is on in the background while she folds laundry, does dishes, or packs lunch for the next day. The problem for Sarah was that even during her rest time, her mind was not resting. It was still churning on all cylinders. She would watch Netflix while she planned what she was going to say in tomorrow's meeting, made a grocery list in her head, or strategized what she could do to fix all sorts of problems that after a few coaching sessions, we agreed weren't even hers to solve. When we live in our heads—in planning, worry, or anxiety—it's difficult to ever recover from emotional exhaustion. Our minds trap us in constant motion—and the fear of slowing down literally sends us into paralysis, just as it did for me at the Holiday Inn.

There is an alternative to this fake rest. The one tool that transforms my clients' lives more quickly than anything else is learning there are two types of rest: *numbing rest* and *restorative rest*. The amount of time you partake in each will make all the difference in how you experience happiness in life. No matter what your job, income, or family unit looks like, the way you feel in your day-to-day life comes down to the amount of restorative versus numbing rest you are getting.

Want to take stock yourself? Consider these example activities and highlight the ones you have done in the last week.

NUMBING REST	RESTORATIVE REST
• Social media • Netflix or TV • Wine, caffeine, or sugar • Scrolling on phone or constant messaging • Shopping or online shopping • Attending happy hours or events we don't want to go to • Anything to escape our pain	• Walks or time in nature • Bath • Meditation • Journaling • Quality time with people you love • Moving your body • Doing something with your hands • Practicing a hobby • Playing a sport • Connecting with loved ones

Just like breathing and eating, restorative rest is a core human need. However, unlike breathing, restoration is not automatic. It is a skill that must be learned. Restorative rest is anything that is nourishing, energizing, and leaves us happier than when we started.

Before we worked together, Sarah only "stopped to rest" when her tank was on empty. By then, she had no mental energy to think of what would feel restorative. Restorative rest requires intention and choosing, something that is very difficult to do from a state of depletion. But here is the scary part. It's at this moment when we push past our energetic "output threshold" for the day that we frequently turn to numbing rest. We've worked hard, and now we're in "check out and chill" mode, pouring a glass of wine and scrolling Instagram before we even consider there could be another way to spend this time. What felt like your noble hard work throughout the day is now leaving you in a life-threatening state of denying yourself essential restorative rest.

Don't get me wrong, I think there is a time for enjoying a good episode (or three) of *Emily in Paris* and uncorking a bottle of champagne from Champagne (if you're confused, Google it). But when the checking-out, disassociating patterns of numbing rest become your go-to (or worse, your only tool in the box), you are a train heading for a crash on the tracks of life. Life is a dance between outputs (tasks, responsibilities) and inputs (energetic regeneration). When you neglect the inputs, it's no wonder you feel burned out.

What we really need is a deep, healing, *truly* restorative rest. We need permission to love on the parts of our life that are screaming for attention. We need to sink into spaciousness, connection, and pleasure without guilt or shame. And mostly, we want to feel good. The catch is when we try to feel good through numbing rest, we're cheating ourselves. We must honor our need for restorative rest the same way we honor commitments to our boss, relatives, or friends. We need to give ourselves a big, fat permission slip to come back into alignment with our highest needs, wants, and desires.

ENTER SOULCATION

Welcome to Your Soulcation. It's time you gave yourself permission to feel good again.

How does it feel to hear these words? Do you sense an ease wash over your body, as if you're receiving something you've wanted for years but always felt was just out of reach? My guess is yes, because your body knows you need a Soulcation, long before your mind has registered exactly what the hell that even means. Let's be honest. Most of you purchased this book without making the effort to Google the word. Why? Because your soul wants a Soulcation—and your mind knows it.

As a recovering scientist, I have the temptation to immediately serve up an expert definition for Soulcation on a silver platter. It's human that whenever we come across a new idea, our brain immediately wants to categorize it, organize it amongst similar things, tie a nice bow on top, and move on. But let me you warn against doing this—as the mystery of Soulcation holds the power to change you. The specifics don't really matter. Everyone's Soulcation will be vastly different. In fact, it's this uniqueness that makes the medicine of Soulcation so potent.

Soulcation is a way of being. It's a lifestyle and essence for how you can design your life around rhythms of restoration that will carry you through all seasons of life. Soulcation is an invitation away from numbing and towards playfulness, lightness, and restorative rest on a daily basis. It is the grand permission slip to swim in the possibility of your needs, wants, and desires before you leave your world to take care of anyone else's. And most of all, Soulcation is the sacred process of slowing down, so you can break the patterns that are keeping you trapped in emotional exhaustion and create a life that feels good—day in and day out, one meeting and one grocery trip to the next. Anything else (dare I say?) is not fully living.

The magic of Soulcation comes by way of *possibility*. The cold, hard truth is it's rarely your work ethic or capacity blocking you from your dream life—it's your imagination. What if instead of chugging along on the path that appears laid out for you, there was another way of moving forward? One where you honored your deepest desires and took action toward the big, crazy dream you've never said out loud that has been simmering inside you for years?

What if you could actually live a life where you had enough time for YOU?

How would it feel in your body to wake up to work that felt energizing, a calendar that felt manageable, and a deep knowing that you had enough time to do activities the old version of you only did on vacation?

What if you found yourself in a life that wasn't so full to the brim you could breathe, nap, and dance your way throughout the day without guilt?

What if pursuing your crazy, big dreams were only possible from a place of spaciousness and rest?

This is the invitation and the grand opportunity of Soulcation. If restoration is the *outcome*, Soulcation is the *way*. It's the way to prioritize self and design a life with your own unique cocktail of nourishing, restorative rest.

Before I believed in Soulcation, the mental chatter of rationality constantly stole my joy—and my openness to this possibility. If I couldn't come up with a clear path from A to B, I wouldn't even try. It kept me safe, but also distant from the feelings of peace, lightness, and ease I longed to feel in my everyday life. That's why I'd be doing you a disservice if I don't say this:

Dear new Soulcationer, I know you're trying oh so hard.
But Soulcation is the path you haven't considered yet.

You don't need another to-do list or workshop. The real work is to sit in the possibility of what else could be—without immediate answers or actions, but with hope, curiosity, and exploration. As a woman who lived far too many years of her life stuck in what I *should* be doing, I'm here to say it's in the possibility of what you *could be* doing that you will find healing.

When I quit my job at the Gates Foundation and set off on my own solo adventure, as I mentioned briefly and will share more about soon, I had a chance to meet women all over the world and ask them what made them happy. And what I heard surprised me. The women with the most freedom, joy, and peace were not the ones with the most money or the finest wardrobes or the most house help. The women I met with the most peace were the ones who gave themselves the permission to choose pleasure and rest in their everyday lives, well before they felt like they had "arrived" or achieved their goals. They spoke at length about the things that helped them feel this way: a bath every night, spending the first hour of their day in a gratifying morning routine, taking an afternoon nap, simplifying and streamlining their work, cooking dinner slowly with a nice glass of wine, not worried about having to go anywhere or do anything afterwards. Most people only let themselves do these things on vacation. But clearly it doesn't have to be this way.

Herein lies a fundamental principle of Soulcation:
You need to use happiness as the way, not the result.

STOP SHAMING YOURSELF

You might be thinking, "This sounds all well and good, Mel, but where do I start? What can I, someone without much time or money, do to kickstart my own Soulcation?"

You start just like you would start anything else. By diverting your attention from *what is* CURRENTLY and connecting with what *could be* IN THE FUTURE. And in order to do this, you need to overcome the first barrier to Soulcationing: self-shaming. When we first begin contemplating more rest, most of us have some sort of run-in with shame. Shame is a painful feeling caused by the consciousness of wrong or foolish behavior. But that's the catch—at first *rest likely will feel foolish*. And we are wired to steer clear of foolish things. For many of us, we are so used to treating rest as a reward, something we give ourselves only *after* we've achieved something, that it feels seemingly impossible to give ourselves rest *just because we need it*. We are our own worst enemies. We become the ungenerous gatekeepers of the very thing our soul desperately needs.

Trying to "should" your way into this Soulcation way of being isn't going to work. No life hack, new calendar management system, or weekend away is going to grant you access to the mindset and essence of giving yourself rest when you need it. You can't keep "shoulding" your way through life and expect a different outcome than you have now. Sister, you have to cash in your chips and play an entirely different game altogether.

That is why Soulcation starts by replacing your "Should" List with what I call a "Happy List." How come? When we're experiencing emotional exhaustion, we need a mental bus stop of sorts—a way to escape the self-created shame cycle of "should" weighing us down. We need to know we can stop the bus, do something that makes us feel good, and find some relief. This is why the very first step of my daily Soulcation Workbook (available at https://takeasoulcation.com) involves creating a Happy List, which is a collection of things you love to do on vacation that hold the possibility of bringing you relief. What makes you ridiculously happy?

I speak to too many women who aren't exactly sure how to answer this question. They let this question go unanswered until their kids go to school, or leave the house, or they retire. Sure, we all want healthy families, meaningful friendships, and a trip to the spa every so often. But somewhere along the way we got so busy that we forgot to deeply explore WHAT WE REALLY WANT and what *could* be possible if we really gave voice to our dreams. This is why there is so much power in a list of things that *could* be possible and *could* make you happy. It's okay not to know at first, but Soulcation is the work of looking inward to find out. Here are some questions I ask my clients as we work on curating their own personalized Happy Lists:

- What do you like doing on vacation? (Or what *did* you do on your last vacation?)
- If you could go on your dream solo vacation, what types of activities would be involved?
- If an appointment was unexpectedly canceled and you had an extra hour in your day, what would you do with this time to yourself?
- If you could splurge and spend money on yourself, what would you invest in?
- What did you most enjoy doing for play and fun when you were a child?

WHY SEX IS BETTER ON VACATION

If you're reading this book, you're likely in the large demographic of people who drop at least some hard-earned cash each year to go on vacation. You spend your time deciding whether you want to go to the beach or the mountains next summer, and then live off the anticipation of this upcoming trip.

Have you ever stopped to ask yourself why you do this?

The short answer, I would guess, is because vacations feel good. But why they make you feel good is a more complicated question, and the secret to unlocking a life you don't need a vacation *from*.

On vacation, we give ourselves permission to do nothing, be lazy, and choose our favorite things *without guilt*. We willingly silence the voice in our head that is always whispering (or screaming): *DO MORE*. Vacations, at their psychological essence, afford us the mental break we so desperately need to do nothing and simply be.

Take vacation sex as an example. Whether it be a dreamy beach or simply a hotel room in the next town over, many of my clients report leaving home makes them more in the mood for sex. At home, their minds spin with things to do. Each evening, there's the need to do the dinner dishes, make sure the urgent emails are answered, and prepare the coffee for the next morning. By the time they get through this evening task list, their internal gas tank is at zero and they have no emotional capacity left for sex. Sometimes they engage—of course. However, as one client said to me, "Sex was too often a fast and furious box-checking exercise, done for my husband's pleasure, not mine. My body (and my vagina) would be present, but my mind would be elsewhere."

Then vacation came. It would take a few days for her to get into "vacation mode." There would be a bathtub and a nice robe and breakfast available until 11:00 a.m., and she wouldn't feel guilty or like she "should be doing something" to keep up with her life back home. She discovered how much she liked morning sex on vacation—soft, slow, not in any hurry. She needed the mental spaciousness of not having anyone else's worlds or demands pulling her out of herself (or her body) to experience the real, juicy pleasure of sex. For most women, *good sex is not hurried sex.*

That's what I want you to realize about your life. By actually doing the thing that feels completely against everything you've learned—slowing down, creating space, taking a Soulcation, you will start to experience a tingling sensation of fully living in your everyday life. This is what I want you to think about when you think about Soulcation: sex on vacation, but for mind, body, and soul. It doesn't require a trip to Paris or some elaborate girls' weekend where you stay up late fixing each other's problems. The benefits of a Soulcation don't require money at all. In fact, play, rest, and pleasure (rather than hard work, external validation, and people-pleasing) can be the pathway to transformation.

Too many of us wait until disaster hits (the cancer diagnosis comes, the marriage fails, we get passed up for the promotion we've been sacrificing for) to start meeting our own needs. Soulcation requires a leap into this immediate need-meeting way of living NOW. But if you are brave enough to take the leap, I'm here to say a net will appear, and the currents of this new *Soulcation path* will carry you the rest of the way.

Real life change is only possible by facing the things fueling your emotional exhaustion, not by numbing them. Too many of us try to heal inner wounds through external action, when what we really need is to slow down, get still, and feel (rather than think) our way to the next step. We need the way of Soulcation. And we need to channel the ethos of vacation sex into every inch of our lives.

CHAPTER 4: CHECKING ALL THE BOXES BUT YOUR OWN

My mom died on a sunny Wednesday in July, six months after I found myself unable to *truly rest* in that Holiday Inn hotel room. She made herself breakfast the day before, toast with cinnamon and sugar sprinkled on top, just like she made when we were kids. We sat on the back deck with cozy blankets on our laps and talked all about my brother's wedding, which was four days away. Then that night the cancer started its final rampage. Twelve hours later she was gone. She was fifty-four years old.

My mom's death was both unplanned and planned. We knew she was dying, but we didn't know when. And when "when" came, it unleashed an ugly storm. It had been nearly ten months of doctor's appointments, hospital admissions, dressing wounds, administering home IV meds, and staying by her side to distract her from the phantom pain from her leg amputation. My life had been put on pause. I was juggling dozens of balls, but I was a ghost of a human. Sure, I let people bring over a meal here and there, but my life had ballooned into an unmanageable cocktail of things. Yet inside my balloon, I was stuffing down the anger I felt about carrying this emotional weight, too afraid of what might emerge if I let myself feel it all.

The Friday night two days after Mom died was the first time I was both back in my own home, and alone with my husband. We had returned to our apartment to collect the mail, water the plants, and make arrangements for the funeral. I thought I would sit on my couch with a cup of tea and write a love letter to Mom, but reality was totally different. Instead, I stormed through the house screaming at Brock, "You didn't help me! Why did you so often refuse to take shifts at the hospital or cook dinners so I could have a break? I'm so mad at you." I rushed into the closet and started throwing everything—his clothes, socks, shoes, anything I could find—towards him. "How dare you keep having fun and enjoying life when my life stopped?" I was full-on in his face, screaming at the top of my lungs. I ran to the bathroom, the only room in our apartment that had a lock on the door and started ugly sobbing.

I had worked so hard helping to manage my mom's healthcare, taking on the emotional labor for our family, and maintaining my role as the primary breadwinner. I missed my mom. I wanted the pain to go away. I wanted to play big in life and feel good. I didn't know how to make it through this emotional tunnel. I was helping everyone else, but in all these months of crisis, I hadn't given much thought on how to help ME through emotional exhaustion.

PATRIARCHY STRESS DISORDER

Women and girls are subconsciously taught from the time we're young that a core part of being female is taking care of other people's needs. When we emerge from the womb, our mother is the first person we want love (and breastmilk!) from. So, it's no surprise then that as we grow up, we learn to mimic our mother's behavior patterns as a means to finding love and acceptance from others. We watch the women in our lives, and we attempt to become like them. In this manner, the female identity of emotional labor is passed down from generation to generation.

Don't hear me wrong. As I said before, I believe one of our biological superpowers as women is to emotionally nurture. We give. We serve. We support. We care a whole damned lot. We make lists of all the things that need to be done at work, at home, and for our people. Our eyes constantly scan the horizon of our loved ones' lives for unspoken needs. And we are pros at swooping in to meet a need before anyone ever notices something was wrong to begin with. It is what makes women so capable of such success in the workplace and is literally what keeps humans proliferating.

However, if you've ever found yourself throwing shoes and screaming out in anger about the invisible labor and emotional burden you carry (like I did), I'm here to say first, that it's always wrong to throw things and you probably owe someone an apology; and second, the root cause of your anger is not solely your fault, sister. There is a generational heritage at play holding you back and giving you a starting disadvantage in the game of rest. Without first healing it, we cannot fully claim a life we don't need a vacation from.

This collective generational heritage is called Patriarchal Stress Disorder. This term has been coined by the brilliant therapist Valerie Rein, who authored the book, *Patriarchy Stress Disorder: The Invisible Inner Barrier to Women's Happiness and Fulfillment.*[6] In it she describes how our shared trauma (Patriarchy Stress) keeps us thinking it's our fault we can't do it all. She writes:

> *"Millions of women feel stuck trying solve their most frustrating problems that they've tried everything to fix, so they can break through to a new level of success in their work, relationships, and health. It's not their failure. There's a missing piece in therapy, coaching, peak performance,*

leadership development, personal growth, and self-help. Without it, we cannot fully heal and claim the lives we desire.

This missing piece is a condition that has us playing smaller than we are, focusing on surviving instead of thriving, being out of touch with our true desires and needs—let alone ways of getting them met. It affects our minds, bodies, nervous systems, choices, and actions.

It's as pervasive as it is invisible. And it's not our fault. This elephant in the room—it is called Patriarchy Stress Disorder® (PSD).

What is that? I'm glad you asked. You see, it's never been safe to be a woman. Historically, it's been particularly unsafe to be an outspoken, attractive, successful woman. Our nervous systems carry the intergenerational trauma of the war on women's bodies, minds, and spirits, our freedoms, choices, and desires.

The more a woman breaks through the inner and outer glass ceilings and grows in her visibility and success, the more her nervous system drives up its hyper-activation, hyper-vigilance:

Our nervous system perceives increased success as increased threat.

Let this sink in for a moment.

Patriarchal Stress Disorder is an upper limit problem—we don't feel safe to let ourselves be happy, and to enjoy all the play, rest, and pleasure that is our birthright. We essentially are afraid to step into the success we deserve. It is also a problem that didn't start with you. Thinking "it's my fault" or "something is wrong with me" is exactly what the patriarchy wants. It keeps you addicted to tending to others' needs before your own, and it keeps you doubting that life could be easy.

Everyone in a female body carries this collective trauma because of our lineage, and it is what pulls us to deny our needs, stay small, and ultimately, doubt whether we can really have the success we want. You can do more, switch things up, and even trade out a house, job, or partner for another one—but patriarchal stress will stay hovering over your head. This is what makes the patriarchy strong. It was built to make you doubt you can have what you want, stay silent, and abandon your needs and wants in service of others. The patriarchy works because women subconsciously consent to the system, and we ignore, deny, or suppress parts of ourselves for the sake of those we love. Our love is beautiful—but love wrapped in emotional exhaustion and patriarchal stress is a monster, waiting to rear its ugly head, just as it did for me in that awful fight with my husband.

THE CURE: MEET YOUR OWN NEEDS, SISTER

All my life my mom was sweet, kind, and polite. She did all the classic mom things of her generation. She cooked hot breakfasts, packed lunches, and shuttled me to gymnastics. I knew she had my back—but I never knew what was fully going on under the surface. She never had big feelings and she rarely expressed emotions. She was the person who was "fine" if anyone asked. And Mom was fine with being "fine."

I was the opposite. I had REALLY BIG feelings. They would shoot through my nervous system and awaken every sensation in my body. I couldn't ignore them. Sometimes I couldn't sleep. I would often "get in trouble" because I didn't know what to do with them, so I would act out for attention. Then I would get sent to my room. That bedroom is where I spent most of my childhood, alone with those big feelings. Sadly, I don't have memories of being held or comforted by Mom in that room. Being alone was where people in my family went to "deal with emotions."

I remember the day I lost the election for student body president at my high school. It was devastating. When I got the news, I rushed to the bathroom stall and cried alone through all of lunch. That day my mom came to pick me up, I told her the news with a straight face, and we drove home in silence. By that point I had learned the intensity of my emotions scared my mom, and thus I did everything I could to avoid showing them to her.

I now know I'm a highly sensitive person (HSP), defined as someone with a heightened central nervous system that is more sensitive to physical, emotional, or social stimuli. As an HSP, living in a family that didn't model a healthy expression of emotions for me meant they came out in unhealthy ways. I would yell or throw things just to get someone to pay attention to my feelings. In fact, my tantrum with Brock was a rendition of the same plea I had made time and time again as a child—*to pay attention to me and my feelings.*

Looking back, I see now I built my adult life around fixing everyone else's emotional pain in the hope that someday someone would reciprocate and meet me in mine. I willingly left my world and took care of the wants, needs, and desires of others, *all with the expectation they would come back to my world and do the same.* It was a game of unconscious manipulation. And it was a serious case of codependency.

Codependency at its core is excessively focusing on other people's needs and wants while simultaneously denying your own needs and wants. It can look like loss of identity, ignoring self, putting your own needs last, or refusing to rest. Most codependents are extremely high-functioning and successful, because alas, they know how to get shit done. That's how they have learned to survive—by meeting every need they see. But when we operate in codependency, we numb our feelings and judge them as invalid. We put a smile on our face and distance ourselves from the uncomfortable negative emotions we were never taught how to feel, pretending everything is okay when it's definitely not. It may seem counterintuitive, but this desire to need everyone around you to feel good is at the core of your unhappiness. And the way to feel happy again is to take responsibility for feeling your emotions. Remember, emotions are like tunnels we must travel through in order to be free from them. In order to Soulcation, we must head into the tunnel.

FIGHT FOR YOUR NEEDS LIKE YOUR LIFE DEPENDS ON IT

Let's pause and do an exercise. What are you feeling in this very moment? Scan this list and circle the word or words that ring truest.

- Joy
- Appreciation
- Empowerment
- Freedom
- Love
- Passion
- Enthusiasm / eagerness
- Happiness
- Positive expectation / belief
- Optimism
- Hopefulness
- Contentment
- Boredom
- Pessimism
- Frustration / irritation
- Impatience
- Overwhelm
- Disappointment
- Doubt
- Worry
- Blame
- Discouragement
- Anger
- Revenge
- Hatred / rage
- Jealousy
- Insecurity / unworthiness
- Guilt
- Fear
- Grief
- Desperation / despair
- Powerlessness

Did you circle a positive emotion, such as joy or contentment? Or a negative one, such as overwhelm or grief? Now ask yourself, did you gravitate toward a positive emotion because perhaps those are easier for you to name, or you feel you *should be* feeling that way? As a second step in this exercise, go back and circle the emotion that is the *most difficult* for you to access and feel. Don't overthink this—the point is to recognize the emotional tunnels through which you tend to avoid traveling. And if you're anything like me, my guess is when you have an unmet need, negative feelings arise. Your inner critic kicks into high gear. You don't exactly welcome them with a party. Instead, you judge yourself for simply having these crazy needs. "If I were just doing things right, it wouldn't hurt so bad," you say to yourself, as you turn your attention back to your to-do list.

I call bullshit on this.

Hiding, managing, and denying ourselves permission to feel our negative emotions is what's making us sick. And knowing what emotional tunnels you resist entering is key to defining your path for growth on Soulcation.

YOU CAN'T HEAL WHAT YOU DON'T FEEL

In order to process and heal our emotional wounds, we need two things: radical validation of exactly how we're feeling, and extravagant permission to meet our needs, no matter what.

When we criticize our feelings, needs, and desires, we hide from them. When we turn toward our needs—like me finally turning toward the grief I had bottled up while my mom was sick—we set out on the path to healing. A lot of clients tell me, "Of course, Mel, I feel my feelings." But as we dive in deeper, we often find an ocean of feelings—both from the past and the present—still unfelt. When we start looking into this underworld, I always ask one key question:

What if you walked through life believing your needs were the most holy, sacred, and important things to listen to every day?

If we're honest with ourselves, most of us don't walk through life this way. Why? Because our inner critic—the part inside of us that judges, criticizes, or demeans us—is running the show. A woman with a well-developed inner critic is blocked from connecting with her emotions, let alone meeting her most significant needs. If you want to know whether you listen most to the voice of the inner critic or your voice of self-compassion, see how many in each category resonate below.

VOICE OF THE INNER CRITIC	VOICE OF SELF-COMPASSION
• When I achieve __________, then I will rest. • I have too much to do; I can't possibly pause and take care of myself. • Feeling sad makes me weak; I will pretend like everything is okay. • I can't stop until everyone else is taken care of first. • I'm wasting time by doing all this self-care. I could be using this time to get stuff done and get ahead. • If I don't keep doing things for other people, they won't love me. • My feelings don't matter.	• My needs are valid. • I am not weak for expressing my negative feelings; rather, I am embodying the full breadth of my very being. • The only way to feel the way I want to feel in life is by compassionately acknowledging all feelings when they arise in my body. • I can't ask anyone else to take care of my needs before I take care of my needs.

We can't change the world from a place of self-denial. It's time to take off our masks and embrace the truth. All our denying, numbing, and stuffing down of emotions and needs is keeping us from living.

DO YOU HAVE A LIST FOR YOURSELF?

For the launch of the Soulcation Workbook (available at https://takeasoulcation.com/), I researched how women structure and plan their days. I interviewed dozens of women—from stay-at-home moms to CEOs to digital nomads—and asked them to show me their digital calendars, paper calendars, organization apps, and sticky notes, and walk me through how they coordinated kids' calendars, partners' calendars, vacation calendars, and medical appointments. The evidence was astounding—every one of the women I interviewed honored commitments, showed up on time, and got the majority of the things on their list done before bed. In fact, most of them added new things to their list throughout the day and got those done too. They were experts at keeping everything organized and life spinning. However, the one thing NONE of the women I interviewed had was what I call a Happy List. *Turns out we deploy gusto and radical commitment to doing things for others, but it's a different story when it comes to ourselves.*

I first created a Happy List a few weeks after my mom's death. "You need to prioritize taking time to be with your grief, Mel," my recently hired therapist said at the time. I wasn't going to argue with her. Sure, I needed to grieve the death of my mother, stop the panic attacks, and, yes ma'am, find a way to revive my marriage. That was why I was in her office.

"I know this might sound strange," she said during a session, "but I think what you really need in the wake of this grief is a Happy

List. You need to train your body and mind to believe it's safe to experience pleasure again."

On the heels of my mom's death, I thought she was crazy. *It surely isn't the moment to start indulging in frivolous things like rest, play, and pleasure,* I reasoned to myself. *My to-do list is way too long for that.* Pleasure would come when the debris from this train wreck was cleaned up, and lighting candles around the bathtub seemed like something that could wait. In fact, I couldn't even recall the last time I'd cleaned my bathtub well enough to actually want to sit in it.

"You don't have to believe in this," sweet therapist Susan said to me. "But I beg you to *experiment,"* she finished, drawing upon her knowledge that I was a scientist by training and loved a good experiment. Over the following weeks, she warmed me up to the idea, and together we titled the experiment my Summer of Self-Love (SOSL). The intention was to prioritize *myself* and *my needs* above all the other things and people requiring my attention.

After looking up how much money I had in my savings account to play with, I took out a yellow office pad of paper and wrote "SOSL Happy List" on the top. It started with simple things I could squeeze into normal life: go to yoga, do not work in the evenings, go to bed before 11:00 p.m. Other things were a bit edgier for me—like "buy clothes other than my navy-blue uniform" and "book weekly dinners with girlfriends." I also added "get my nails done every other week, find a massage therapist, sometimes give yourself permission to eat cheese for dinner instead of cooking, and buy yourself gourmet doughnuts each Saturday morning." The last item on the list was the most extravagant: "Go on a solo getaway to Seattle's famous Willows Lodge," a boutique hotel experience featured in all the Northwest travel magazines.

A month later, I drove into the manicured grounds of Willows Lodge with my swimsuit, a journal, and brand-new luxury pajamas (I had upgraded a bit from the Holiday Inn sweatpants situation), ready to curl up and pretend I was a queen for the weekend (rather than the hot mess, anxiety-ridden human I still felt like inside). I ordered farm-to-table crab mac 'n' cheese for dinner, crawled into the high thread count, silky sheet bed, and thanked myself for agreeing to this whole Happy List experiment!

The next morning, my body was stiff. I could hardly roll out of bed. My heart was racing. It was hard to breathe. My pesky anxiety had reared its head and consumed me yet again. As the clock approached 11:53 a.m. (the time of my mom's death), I filled the large spa soaking tub, turned the water as hot as it would get, and crawled in, hoping the hot water would help all my hot, fiery, and uncontrollable anxiety seep out. I dunked my head under the water and surrendered to my body, fully submerged. Lingering there with my eyes closed and no oxygen, for the first time in my life, I wondered what the world would be like if I just never came up for air. *Who would come to my funeral? What would people say about me? All those insane hours I spent working wouldn't even be remembered, would they?*

I did this dance of crying and dunking my head under the water and then crying some more for hours, only interrupting to refill the bathtub when it got too cold. After my tear ducts were emptied, I surprisingly felt better. At Willows Lodge, away from my home (and all the strings and people attached to it) I could finally let loose and cry. I had entered the scary emotional tunnel of grief, and I didn't die. In fact, my stuck grief was starting to move.

Then a thought occurred to me. Maybe ... just maybe ... I should do this more often. I could cry, feel my negative emotions, and not die. In fact, I felt happier afterwards, and I deserved to be happy again. Drying off, I grabbed that same yellow pad of paper I made my SOSL Happy List on and started writing down even more wild things. *If I'm going to really experiment, why not go all in?* I thought. In a moment of stream-of-consciousness inspiration, I wrote down, "Go to Europe." Besides a few conferences for work, I still had never been there for an extended time. Next, I wrote: "Start writing again." I had always loved writing and dreamed of writing a book, although at that point I hadn't even written in my journal in a year. Finally, I wrote, "Stop working." I wasn't sure what deep crevice of my brain that came from: I just knew that the bathtub crying actually felt good, and it only came when I put work away long enough to sit still. No matter how high-stakes my work was, I started to actually see my own life as even higher stakes.

The rest of the afternoon, I sat alone in my room with that yellow notepad. I stared at it in simple wonder. What if I tried to make all these things scribbled on this notepad happen? If I put more effort into trying to be happy than trying to be productive—could I actually make these crazy desires happen?

CHAPTER 5: THE ILLUSION OF HAPPILY EVER AFTER

I woke up to dark Seattle rain clouds that mimicked the heaviness inside me. It had been seven emotionally exhausting months since my mom died. If she had been alive, that week would have been her fifty-fifth birthday and thirty-fifth wedding anniversary. We would have been celebrating with eggs Benedict and cherry pie for breakfast (her favorite) and handwritten cards. That day there were no celebrations and no love notes. Instead, I woke up with an acne breakout, an aching back, and a sense that love was nowhere near.

From the outside, it was just another Saturday. I sat with my cup of coffee at our kitchen table and went about my routine of making a glorious list of things I needed to do for the day: wash the sheets, run to the grocery store, make a dessert for tonight's dinner club, respond to some work emails, go to a marriage counseling appointment, and schedule my next gynecology appointment. On days when the pain of losing Mom threatened to paralyze me, I resorted to my number one coping strategy: getting shit done. None of these things on my list were hot button items, though. I didn't *have* to cook a homemade dessert or schedule my gynecology appointment today. And I sure wasn't required to respond to work emails on Saturday, but I told myself I wanted to do it ... even *needed* to. Moving my way down a list—any list—kept me from having to travel through the emotionally intense tunnel of my mom being gone.

I did what Mel was good at, and moved at lightning speed through my Saturday list, pulling up to our therapist's office just in time. When I walked in, Brock was already seated on one end of the monotone couch that looked like it had been lifted out of my grandma's house. I nodded at him and offered a soft smile.

"Good to see both of you," our therapist, Susan, said. "Mel, I know today is the anniversary of your mom's death. How are you doing, sweet thing?"

"I'm doing fine," I responded. I hoped she read that as, *can we talk about anything else BUT this please?*

"I've been busy at home all day, haven't really had a chance to think about it. But tomorrow the family is all getting together to finally clean out her closet. That's going to be hard," I said in a whisper. "But enough about me, what are we going to work on in today's appointment?" I said, glancing at Brock. We always rotated bringing an issue forward at these sessions, and today was his turn.

"Actually, Mel, I want to read to you an apology letter I've been working on." My jaw dropped and I glanced at Susan in shock. She had encouraged us to write these letters, but we both had been putting them off for weeks, both waiting for the other to be the first to raise the white flag. Brock reached into his backpack and pulled out white paper with printed black ink.

> "Mel, I'm sorry I wasn't there for you during key moments during your mom's death.
> I'm sorry I didn't stay at the hospital when you asked me to.
> I'm sorry for not showing up and helping around the house.
> I'm sorry for not taking the pain your family was going through more seriously.
> I'm sorry for not sitting and being present with you when you were going through so much.
> I'm sorry for not listening more.

> I'm sorry I wasn't available for you.
>
> I'm sorry for not loving you the way you deserve to be loved..."

I teared up. I felt soft, seen, and loved by him for the first time in months, yet I couldn't seem to look directly into his eyes—still in shock these words were finally coming out of his mouth. I gazed out Suzan's office window, the clouds still dark and heavy, rain coming down, and cars making their way through puddles on the road outside. It all felt surreal. *Could his words finally heal me instead of hurt me?*

When he finished, he glanced over at Susan with a knowing gaze. I watched as her eyes also started to tear up. *Therapists aren't supposed to cry. Wait, am I missing something?*

Susan jumped in, "Brock, thank you for sharing this. Mel, before I give you a chance to respond, Brock has one more thing to share with you. Brock, we both know today is a big day. Do you still have something to add?"

"No, I'm ready," he said, leaving me utterly confused. He adjusted his legs to point away from me, and his eyes gazed up towards the ceiling. "Mel, I meant every word of my apology. However, I also have some other news ..."

He looked back down at the paper on his lap. "After lots of thought, I've come to an important decision. I know we have both worked hard to create a marriage where we can both be happy. But I can't do this anymore. Today I will be filing for a divorce. I am thankful for our good times together, but it is clear our marriage is irreconcilable."

*What the f***?!* I choked silently, looking at Susan in complete shock. It felt like my mom's death all over again. One minute everything is normal, and the next the world comes crashing down. Brock was my first boyfriend. I lost my virginity to him on our wedding night, as Christian girls were "supposed" to do. He was the first one I ever said "I love you" to—and in my family and religious upbringing, he was supposed to be the last.

She nodded at me. She knew this was coming. My heart dropped.

Ever since my ugly post-death explosion at Brock, our marriage had been shaky. My feelings of sadness consumed me. Brock didn't know how to enter them. I didn't know how to leave them. We were two humans at a loss for how to find each other underneath the mess. I thought our pulling away was a temporary survival strategy, but it turned out to be the start of another ugly death. I had just lost the first person on earth ever to love me—Mom. Now I was standing at the threshold of losing a second person. A one-two punch.

Too upset to drive, I waited with Susan until Heidi, one of my best friends, arrived to get me. In between piling wet Kleenex on the floor and letting the mascara run down my face, I tried to explain. But I couldn't explain without admitting I had been lying to myself—and to Heidi—for months now. Confessing my marriage was in tatters was the one thing I had spent so much effort trying NOT to do. We had had months of ugly fights. We had stopped date nights and talking about emotional things. We agreed to therapy, but our hearts had already checked out. We put on a front that we were weathering the death of my mom in stride, but the truth was, it was drowning us. Not even Heidi, my best friend at the time, knew how bad things were.

"Another Kleenex please," I said to Heidi after I finally told her as much as I could get out. She reached for the box, noting there were only a few left. "Mel, it's almost 6:00 p.m. Are you hungry?"

"No, not really. But our dinner party," I said.

"Friend, you're in no shape for that. Dinner party is canceled. You're coming home with me."

I sprawled out on Heidi's couch, surrounded now by my three closest friends, all doting over me and eating takeout pizza. Heidi brought a wet, cold towel for my forehead and handed me a slice. "Just try to take one bite ..." she pleaded.

Curled up in the fetal position, my mind was racing—already in full-on problem-solving mode. *What secret was he hiding? How could I get him to talk? And more importantly, how could I talk him out of this decision?*

I need to find a way to make this all go away.

I need to find a way to make this all go away.

I need to find a way to make this all go away.

My mind churned with this thought, trying to find a ploy to both temporarily protect our image and change his mind. I had to fix this. That was *who I was*. Mel the master fixer. I had a story in my head of how my life was supposed to go, and that involved staying married, staying in our home, and staying on script. The only way I knew to maintain this story and protect myself from pain was to get Brock to change his mind. Even if I was miserable. Even if I hated his guts some days. Even if our life together kind of sucked. I didn't want to go through the tunnel of grieving my marriage. That tunnel felt too scary, dark, and dangerous to enter. As I fell asleep in my best friend's guest room alone that night, I promised I would fight with all my strength to keep the marriage alive. *That's what good girls do,* I thought. *We tolerate pain and never give up.*

THE PERFECTION SPELL

When we don't want to travel through life's inevitable emotional tunnels, we have another option: pretend the tunnels don't exist. The benefit of this avoidance is we don't have to sit in our dark, uncomfortable feelings. However, the cost is we will never reach higher peaks in our life, as we know by now not traveling through emotional tunnels is what leads to emotional exhaustion, anxiety, and burnout. The obsession with perfection is an all too common—and socially acceptable—way to avoid tunnels. Perfectionism, defined as unreasonable expectations that negatively impact your self-worth and ability to enjoy life, presents like a chronic disease. It creeps up on you slowly, until the pain gets bad enough.

I know I'm neither the first nor the last person to find herself curled up in a fetal position gasping for air after spending too many years pretending her marriage was fulfilling, when the truth was it wasn't. For me, at the time of my divorce, I was still deeply religious. I lived by the standards for marriage outlined by my church, which defined success as the marriage lasting forever (rather than the happiness and expansion one received from it). Self-sacrifice was celebrated. *So who am I to complain about not getting my needs met?* I would tell myself.

Regardless of what cocktail of expectations and standards you have pieced together from religion, society, or family, we all have them. They help us feel in control of our lives. Deep down we may know they are unrealistic. We may even jokingly admit we are a perfectionist. Yet just like I did, we may do nothing about it until crisis hits.

ENTER THE TUNNEL ... ASK FOR HELP

My watch showed it was 11:45 a.m., still fifteen minutes to go until the end of our team meeting. The morning had included calls with the government of Namibia and the African Malaria Leaders Alliance, and a brainstorm session about what to include in an upcoming memo to Bill and Melinda Gates. Despite the urgent emails in my inbox, I had to go. It would take at least fifteen minutes to exit the Gates Foundation glass fortress, maneuver through security, and travel by Uber to my first support group meeting. As I got ready to quietly make an exit, I tossed my expensive watch in my purse, mentally preparing myself to transition from boss-woman Mel to a version of me that required the most surrender and humility of my life. Despite the story I had in my head, there was one secret I had been hiding: I had hit my husband. Underneath my good Christian girl exterior, I had a mother lode of pent-up anger. It had happened months ago during a fight, and I hadn't done anything about it. That is—until now.

It was only a week since the news he was leaving. I signed myself up for this support group as a bid to win him back, but it quickly became the entry point to the dark emotional tunnels I had been avoiding. The curriculum was similar to Alcoholics Anonymous' 12-step program. It required you admit you had a problem, take radical responsibility, seek accountability, and commit to change. According to its website, the program was based on the philosophy that "in order to heal, you must start by telling the truth to yourself." I was scared shitless.

I had been raised in a deeply evangelical home. We talked about the good things and bypassed negative things with phrases like, "God is in control. It will all work out." But with divorce looming, I couldn't help but wonder, *if God was good, and if I had spent so many years trying to be good for Him, why in the world did I feel so damn bad on the inside?*

I climbed the staircase of the old brick building where our group meetings were held. We started with introductions. Covered in tattoos, Sally introduced herself by saying, "I was ordered by court to be in group. So, here I am." Next to her was Martha, who told us she lived on and off the streets and was struggling to keep a job. She recently got the news her husband would get full custody of her two children due to her violence, and she hadn't eaten for days over the news. Then there was Laurie who told us, "My husband didn't come home last night, and I am so angry about his mischief I punched a pillow for a full hour." These women didn't seem ashamed to talk about the dark, ugly underbellies of their lives. This was the only domestic violence group for women in Seattle I had found on Google, but hearing all the introductions made me realize how deeply angry I was, and also how much anger likely lives silently inside the souls of women.

As the weeks went on, I let my guard down. Sally, Martha, Laurie, and the other six women started to become friends in a way I hadn't experienced before. Around our shared table, I verbalized the rage I had learned I was capable of, and that scared me to my core. I talked about that night my mom went to hospice, when my husband told me he had to leave my side for another band trip. I exploded into a raging ball of fire and hit him right there in the car.

I talked about how much screaming went on behind closed doors. I talked about how Brock had changed his mind about having kids after we were far along into the fertility process, and how my womb hadn't stopped rumbling in anger. Most of all, around that table I admitted I had a problem, and fully owned up to my deep-seated capacity for destruction.

By listening to other women put words around their darkest, ugliest feelings, I slowly started to understand that own place in my soul. I noticed how the physical sensations of anger showed up in my body—a boiling, hot, pressure-cooker feeling. I was angry for a reason—and I had been denying myself the right to look under the lid and explore why.

After my fourth group meeting, I reached out to Brock to share what I was learning. He informed me he had filed the official paperwork, hired a lawyer, and even created a spreadsheet of every spoon, plate, and bedsheet in our house to be divided. I was getting divorced, and had no choice but to enter the dark, painful tunnel in front of me all alone. The weight of panic, burnout, internalized capitalism, patriarchy stress, perfectionism, and religion were pulling me under. It was time for a Soulcation.

CHAPTER 6: LEAP AND THE NET SHALL APPEAR

I was well into my Summer of Self-Love, and it felt both selfish and deliciously wonderful. Despite my spa trips and cheese dinners, the pressure at work was intensifying, and my panic attacks continued. I spent weeks in therapy with sweet Susan talking though what I called my "early onset midlife crisis."

"Susan, I have my dream job. I love the Gates Foundation, I love the mission, and I love my team. I'm about to get promoted. I never thought I would have it this good," I would repeat. "I just don't like how I feel inside my body. My stomach is in knots, I work well into the night and still don't feel like it's enough, and I haven't felt a sense of slowness and peace, well ... in years."

"Mel, I can see you want a long break from work. What if you gave yourself exactly what you wanted?" Susan posed one day.

Her words felt like a galactic rebellion in my body.

What if I gave myself exactly what I wanted?

"Like quit my job, you mean?"

"Don't think about it as quitting," she said. "Think of it as saying yes to yourself."

I had come to believe anything good had to involve sweat and tears. Internalized capitalism still had a tight grip on me. *I had no idea how to give myself exactly what I wanted.*

"Here I go," I said to myself as I looked in the mirror, as my mind flashed back to my pale body submerged in the Willow's Lodge bathtub—equally wanting and not wanting to come up for air. It had been six months since Brock filed the divorce paperwork. The clock on the Gates Foundation wall struck 5:00 p.m. Almost all my coverup had worn off, and the red acne and dark grief circles were visible under my eyes. After a full-day workshop inside a windowless room, it was time for my end of the day meeting with Philip, my director. We pulled open the thick glass doors and took a seat in the "campus heart"—the foundation's quaint outdoor courtyard.

"Philip, I want to talk to you about my role on the team," I started, pretending like this was going to be a run-of-the-mill conversation. "It looks like we have all the presidential signatures to officially endorse the next round of funding to the eight southern African countries," I said. He nodded.

"I'm very pleased with how this is going," he affirmed.

Next, he leaned back in the oversized courtyard chair, crossed his arms, and in a knowing way said, "Mel, all this is good news. But I know this year has been hard with your mom dying. Can we pause a moment and talk about how YOU are doing?" My heart dropped. *There is no easy way to communicate I'm not doing well.*

"Philip, a few months after Mom died, Brock left me." The word "left" lingered in the air.

"At first, I thought it would be temporary. But he's gone, Philip. Our divorce has been finalized."

My eyes fought back tears as I went on, "Philip, the only thing going well in my life is work. I can feel the momentum. I wholeheartedly believe in your new strategy and the impact it will have in the world."

Gosh, it's freakin' hard to say this out loud when now I'm not even sure if this is the right decision.

"But ..."

Again, there was more awkward silence.

"Philip, I need some time. I don't know what I'm going to do next, but I need to be fully in this loss—and the only way I know how is to give myself a break."

He looked me in the eyes, and we sat in silence even longer. After a few more seconds, he nodded sympathetically, then gently repeated my words back to me, "So a break, huh?"

I wished ALL I needed was a vacation.

"Philip, I need to quit. I've reached the end of myself—and I think finding myself is going to require finding the girl not addicted to work."

I couldn't hold back the teardrops anymore. Then I saw his eyes water along with mine.

"I'm going to take some time. Then figure out what's next."

"Date?" he uttered, gently and quietly as if I had all the time in the world at my disposal.

"Soon," I said back. "I've planned a long vacation to kick things off. I leave exactly one month from today."

"Go," he said, with zero hesitation. "For the entire month. Whatever you need. Then come back and we will give you a proper farewell."

That night I arrived home to an email from him titled, "Sabbatical." Inside the body of the email included a short message:

> *I'm sorry for everything you're going through, Mel. I want you to know how incredibly supportive of this season of rest I am for you. My wife took a sabbatical last year and it changed everything for her. I'm confident it will for you too. For choosing rest, you have my utmost respect.*
>
> *With Love,*
> *Philip*

THE BEST INVESTMENT YOU'LL EVER MAKE IS IN YOURSELF

When I told my financial planner, Jason, that I was going to quit my job, sell my belongings, and travel solo around the world for an undetermined amount of time, I was met with intense skepticism. Jason would have wildly approved of me buying a house, aggressively putting more towards retirement, or even investing in bitcoin. But to spend what amounted to a down payment on rest, healing, and experimentation with what I wanted—without any guaranteed ROI—got major pushback. I had taken a sizeable financial hit from the divorce, and his advice was to save money, not spend it. However, something in me had this feeling that if I didn't take a pause now, I would work all the way to retirement. And if I did that, I couldn't help but wonder, *what might I miss out on? Could real security come not from owning a home, but rather from doing the work to learn how to be at home in myself?*

Even after I fired Jason and hired a new financial planner, there were a flood of questions from my well-meaning father, extended relatives, and even close friends. After dozens of therapy sessions with Susan talking through this decision, I was committed to my leap, but it sent ripples through the status quo of the relationships closest to me.

Soulcation is based on the belief we all form our lives around the pursuit of safety, mattering, and belonging. They are core human needs, and it's normal for us to gravitate to where we feel safe, where we matter to others, and where we belong to a tribe or community bigger than ourselves. We all find "our people"—whether it be boss-babe people, stay-at-home-mom people, or beach-bum surfer people, and tend to stick close to their side. The status quo of the collective reinforces individual benefit, and we never stop to consider who we would be if we let certain identities fall away.

In rushing to get our needs for belonging met as quickly as possible, we too often find ourselves in a life that feels safe, yet not fully alive. We all huddle together and validate one another's choice to stay on the shore because no one wants to be the first one to leap. We tolerate the same identity, the same shore, and the same patterns for years. Sometimes we look up and gaze out to the horizon of new possibilities. Yet the people that love us the most—and whose voices we have come to trust—can be the first to remind us how grateful we should be for the life on shore. They get something out of us being on shore. *You* get something out of being on shore. And questioning the shore's value starts to loosen the sand beneath everyone's feet. Your shoremates sense your new curiosity and may start to pull back the quotient of safety, mattering, and belonging they offer you. You freak out. Your nervous system goes bananas.

It's easy to stay. But it's transformative to leap.

YOUR NEW LIFE IS GOING TO COST YOU YOUR OLD ONE

It's true what the businessman John A. Shedd said: "A ship in harbor is safe—but that is not what ships are built for." You can feel safe in the shallow waters of the harbor. Or you can leave the harbor in search of true fulfillment and leap. Here is what I know about leaving the harbor and leaping.

A leap costs you the only identity you know now.

A leap costs you the humans you call friends now.

A leap costs you feelings of comfort.

A leap costs being understood.

A leap costs you a breakdown.

A leap is guaranteed to come with suffering.

And a leap costs you your safety, mattering, and belonging.

It is scary as hell, but in my research and experience, it is the only way to transition from a life sourcing safety, mattering, and belonging externally to one sourcing these core needs from within. To change your life requires you to change your identity. And this, soul sister, requires you to change the way you find safety, mattering, and belonging in the world.

My official last day at the Gates Foundation was set for Halloween weekend and it coincided with our annual meeting in New Orleans. I wore a recently purchased (thank you, SOSL) leopard-print dress as my "last day of work" outfit—a symbol that at minimum I could leap out of my navy-blue uniform. As I walked to the conference center at 8:00 a.m., glitter, beads, and colorful wigs lined the New Orleans sidewalk. I could hear live music drifting out from the bar around the corner, and there were still a few dedicated Halloween partiers roaming the streets, too buzzed to go home. *What would it be like to have this type of fun?* I wondered. *Do I really have the better life, all buttoned up and walking to a board meeting on Halloween Friday? What would it be like to let loose like that?*

I arrived in the large boardroom, adorned with nameplates for the VIPs and notebooks with the gold and blue Gates Foundation logo. I took a seat along the back edge of the room, from which the staff observed this meeting each year. For the next eight hours, I listened while experts debated issues and gave advice. However, for the first time in nearly seven years I didn't care anymore. Or maybe I was finally giving myself permission not to care.

Back at my hotel room, I replaced my leopard-print dress with skin-tight black pants, a cropped black shirt, and a red crab hat. Walking down to the lobby, I met up with my two other crab twins: Gates Foundation Director, Philip, and colleague and friend Abi. After a pre-game gin and tonic, we walked toward Bourbon Street. My work was done. A deep, full, *done* done. For the first time in my life, there were no more emails or meetings or follow-ups. I was jobless—with an empty calendar and no responsibility to wake up to in the morning. I used to only dream about what this would be like, but now I was done, and it felt miserably empty and scary.

Glued together as a crab family, we made our way down Bourbon Street towards our prized destination—New Orleans' oldest dive karaoke bar. We walked into a smoky sauna of a room, already full of familiar team faces jammed under the disco ball and drinking cheap beer (as we had learned to do in Africa).

I looked down at my phone out of habit, addicted to checking work email while at a bar waiting for my drink. Abi grabbed my shoulders and pushed me into the crowd, "Relax, Mel. You're done. It's time to have fun now." Then before I could overthink it, I was up on stage with her, belting out "I Want it That Way" like a true Backstreet Boy. The 1990s songs continued, and perhaps for the first time in a decade, I actually had fun without the undercurrent of mental chatter reminding me of all I had to do the next day.

At 3:00 a.m. my broken heart was being wrapped in the sweetest, drunkest, bear hug goodbye finale—the team singing "9 to 5" by Dolly Parton. As we stepped outside onto Bourbon Street to make our way home, Philip put his arm around me and said, "Mel, freedom looks good on you."

"Thank you," I responded, catching a glimpse of a full moon. "You're right. Maybe it does."

LEAP INTO SELF-TRUST

When it comes to leaping, there are *real leaps* and *fake leaps*. I'd be the last to ever call anyone's bluff for pulling a fake leap. And frankly, that's the thing with fake leaps: you wouldn't need me to. You can recognize that it isn't the move you really need when you're making it. When the costs are high, you cringe and think, "I'll leap out of *anything but that (insert job, relationship, home, whatever).*" Sure, there are *fake leaps* that inch you forward, but you know deep down what scale of leap would make the greatest change for you. That's the *real leap*.

Don't get me wrong. Ordering books and setting up coffee dates with smart people can support your growth and learning. But that's not leaping. The thing that propels you from incremental transformation to radical transformation is setting out down a path that is calling to you but is unseen and untested. You don't know the route yet. You haven't yet learned that you are your own best teacher.

The *real leap* (and this is the reason so few people do it) requires that we leave what we *currently* source our safety, mattering, and belonging from (our work, partnership, circle of friends, religious community, or net worth). The reason a leap is so powerful—and will change your life—is that in the free fall, you learn you can source your safety, mattering, and belonging from inside yourself. Take a deep breath and read that sentence again. That's the *real* problem I've been waiting to tell you. At a psychological level, your emotional exhaustion isn't coming from one particular job or relationship or even too few vacation days (as if you can exchange one job or partner out for another and the pain will go away). The deeper truth is you are unconsciously using these things to source some portion of your safety, mattering, and belonging in the world. And until you solve that problem, you're never going to have a life you don't need a vacation from.

If externally sourcing what you have the capability to curate from within is the problem, radical self-trust is the solution. We all know the feeling of being betrayed by someone we love, whether in a romantic relationship, friendship, or work situation. After a betrayal, we walk through the world on edge, with far less trust in others and ourselves. We are deeply hurt. And we resort to various forms of self-protection to make the hurt go away.

Self-betrayal is one of the most universal forms of self-protection. It's a coping mechanism that we usually pick up early in life. Self-betrayal is when we give up on our wants, needs, and desires either because we don't believe they're valid, or we don't believe it would ever be possible to have them met. It is at work whenever we:

- Numb or deny our feelings
- Judge ourselves or others
- People-please
- Hide parts of ourselves from others
- Don't honor our needs
- Don't speak up
- Go against our values
- Make others responsible for our happiness, safety, or need for belonging.

As we grow from children to adults, self-betrayal can often be disguised as self-control. It manifests in over-giving, over-caretaking, and a hyper sense of responsibility. We use self-betrayal as a coping strategy to distance ourselves from the heartbreak, pain, and discomfort we were never taught as children how to be in a relationship with. We think something is wrong with us, and so we cut off these parts of ourselves. Self-betrayal becomes the autopilot of our lives.

Take Stella and Monica. Both women suffer significantly from a lack of self-trust, even though they don't recognize it yet.

Stella's Story

Stella comes home from work after a long day at the office. Tonight is the one night a week her husband picks up the kids and takes them out for pizza, so she can have some time to herself. She is looking forward to drawing a bubble bath, lighting a candle, and reading a book without interruption. However, on the drive home her friend Kelley calls and starts venting about a big fight she had with her husband the night before, clearly upset and fearing a possible divorce. While Stella is clear on what she really wants, she never wants to be the "bad friend" and reluctantly agrees to break the commitment to herself and stop by Kelley's house instead.

Margaret's Story

Margaret grew up playing piano. She started pounding the keys when she was five, and her heart felt so happy making music. She continued to play all through child-

hood, earning a college scholarship and touring across some of the great concert halls in Europe. However, every Christmas when she returned home her parents pressured her by saying, "You're still majoring in economics, right? Piano is good and all, but we want to make sure you can get a real job after college." As Margaret approached her senior year, she started diminishing the time she spent practicing and took more classes in business. After a few more nudges from her parents, she agreed to take an accounting job in her dad's friend's firm after graduation. Margaret now has three kids, a full-time job, and a piano collecting dust in her spare bedroom. However, in the silent morning hours, she still dreams of what her life would be like if she had kept playing professionally.

While these examples are different in terms of the magnitude of the betrayal, both Stella and Margaret valued the needs and opinions of others more than their own. They had an initial trajectory based on self-trust, but they abandoned it in response to pressure by others to do so. Both examples could be interpreted as "good choices," but now that you know about the self-betrayal problem, you won't be surprised to hear they both sent them down a trajectory of unhappiness. And both choices were rooted in years of conditioning that made the choice almost unconscious.

The frequent yet subtle ways we constantly betray ourselves is why solving the self-betrayal problem feels like such a big leap. You're literally rewiring the operating system you have used since childhood to move through the world. The length of the free fall as well as the size of the net that will catch you will be different for each person, but flipping the switch from self-betrayal to radical self-trust and self-fulfillment is the work of Soulcation. The medicine to your burnout and emotional overwhelm lies in repairing the ways you've failed to trust yourself. And that's what the leap is all about: realizing we can trust ourselves, and we had the power all along to give ourselves exactly what we need.

LEAPING INTO A NEW LIFE

It was my first week without my Gates Foundation work to keep me busy—I did what one does when you're bored, jobless, and feeling a lack of meaning in your life. I signed up to learn trapeze. My Google search told me you needed to be at least six years old (*check*!), wear "flexible" pants (*pretty much live in them now, check*), and not have consumed alcohol the day of class (*fine—I can resist, check*). Friends, breaking news: We can all fly!

When the class started, I was shuffled into an area with what looked like my elementary school's monkey bars for twenty minutes of "ground school." Here I was given simple instructions on how to "chalk up," grip the bar, and then dismount, a fancy term for letting go at exactly the moment when the coach yells, "Release!"

"Flying is really a listening sport," the instructor told the class. "The hardest part is learning when to hold on and when to let go. Most people overthink it. Your job is to let your body lead."

Wow, I thought. *I do everything with my mind first. I don't think I could silence the mind for the life of me.*

Ground school was over, and it was my turn to fly. My sweaty palms gripped the thin, metal ladder, and my hands trembled as I started climbing the four stories to the platform above. *Why did I choose to pay actual money for this again?* When I reached the top, a chiseled and extremely good-looking trapeze performer grabbed my hand and pulled me close. I felt electricity shoot through every inch of my body. It felt both scary and delicious.

How long has it been since I've been held by a man? I wondered, letting memories of Brock flash through my mind. With our bodies close on the thin wood plank, he had me wiggle my toes out slightly past the edge of the plank.

"Now lean your hips forward, past your toes," he said with a firm, confident voice. "Lean more ... more ... more, Mel," he went on. It was only his grip on the back of my waist strap keeping me on the plank. "This is launch position," he said, holding me there and letting my body become aware of this feeling of full surrender. "You know you're ready to launch when you've leaned past the point of feeling secure."

"All right!" he shouted. "On the count of three I'm going to let go."

Nooooo, don't let go!!!! I thought.

"One ... two ... launch," I heard.

All I could do was hang on for dear life. My legs didn't swing. My body froze. I just hung there in terror, dangling like a pencil from the air with no momentum to keep me going.

"Release!" the instructor yelled. I managed to let go with only one hand, too afraid to fall into the net below.

"First time is for fear," he said once I was on the ground and out of the tangled mess of the fishnet. "The second time is for fun."

Hmmmmm. *The first time is for fear*, I repeated to myself.

"Feel your fear," the instructor said to me. "It's the only way you will ever fly."

I nodded and whispered back, "It's scary up here."

"I know, but the best things in life come when you do them scared," he said.

With that, I wiggled my toes over the edge of the plank, pushed my pelvis forward like the Leaning Tower of Pisa, and jumped. I moved my legs this second time and got some momentum. I swung my legs fully onto it, stretched my arms out, and tried to keep them solid and still as I flew through the air, blindly awaiting that moment of contact with the catcher.

Our catcher that day was Roy. His long hair and bulging six-pack told me he was a force of nature. Before assuming his position on the opposite swing, he had come over to the group of us beginners for a pep talk.

"Who has been to Cirque du Soleil?" he asked. "And who thought the flyer was the star of the show? All right, the most important thing you need to remember is the flyer is definitely not the star of the show. The worst thing a flyer can do is to try to catch the catcher. The flyer could break his own wrist by trying too hard. It's the catcher who does everything."

A flyer's job is simply to let the catcher do all the work. "Stretch out your hands like this," Roy demonstrated, "Relax, stay calm, and wait to be caught."

It felt too easy. Too good to be true. *Relying on someone else for your life?*

"That's why you fly with your eyes facing the opposite direction. If you see the catcher, you're more likely to stiffen up, change your position, try to take control. Not seeing where you're going is actually the very best way to keep you loose and free and flying."

My friends, that's the art and science of how you fly. It often doesn't make logical sense or feel comfortable in your body. But leaping out of old identities, patterns, and parts of your life does require trusting there will be someone (or something) to catch you on the other side. It requires taking responsibility for climbing to the highest plank you can reach on your own, scooting your toes to the point of discomfort, and letting go. It involves hours swinging through the air blind and upside down with blood rushing to your brain, stomach churning, heart racing, no line of sight to where you're headed—knowing that actually this feeling is entirely normal, and eventually, your shaky, sweaty palms will meet flesh again, and you will be caught. The body will have guided you home.

It really is true: Leap and the net will appear.

PART II:

WHAT IT TAKES TO SOULCATION

CHAPTER 7: CAN YOU TRUST YOURSELF?

My bones felt like they were about to crack. I was weak, likely owing to the combination of Nyquil, wine, and Nescafé I had consumed in the preceding day traveling from Seattle to Lima, Peru. I was wearing a torn jean jacket, yoga pants, and blue glitter sneakers, with my hair in a high ponytail that screamed, "Just call me Hot Mess Mel." The clock above the baggage claim carousel struck 2:00 a.m. as I hauled my suitcase off the belt. *Holy fuck. This. Is. Real. All my earthly possessions are inside this small box on wheels.*

Back in Seattle, with a home, a closet full of belongings, and a fully stocked pantry, it sounded so dreamy to set out on a sabbatical, or what I had now officially dubbed my "Pause." I imagined filling my Instagram feed with glam photos and hashtags like #minimalist and #slowtravel and #bestlifeever. But now I was stinky, hadn't slept in a day, and all I wanted was to be transported back home to my own sheets, memory foam pillow, and familiar bed.

But everything was sold now. I had taken the leap and I could only go forward.

With just my suitcase and smartphone, I stepped out of customs and scanned the wall of Latino men holding handwritten signs and scanned for my name. Nothing. I scanned again. I even walked into the crowd and started yelling in my terrible Spanish, "Conductor para Mel, conductor para Mel?" Still nothing.

My mind started a should-filled anxiety loop. *You should have known better than to book a ticket landing in Peru at 2:00 a.m. You should have set up your international data BEFORE arriving so you could call your driver. You should have written down your address so you wouldn't be stuck like this with no internet and a phone that's about to die. You should. You should. You should.*

I swallowed hard and walked back into the airport. I asked an old man in a police uniform, "Can I borrow your phone? I need to call my driver." He handed me a cheap flip phone, and I dialed the only number I had. On the third ring someone answered: "Hola, coma estás?" I heard.

"Habla Inglés?" I said.

"Nada," I heard back. I handed the phone back to the police officer hoping he would translate. I understood enough of what I heard. "It was a confusion ... I'm an hour away."

He hung up the phone and looked at me sympathetically: "He'll be here at 3:00 a.m." I slid to the floor, tossed my suitcase on its side, and leaned against it, defeated. The airport was eerily quiet. There was only a cleaning crew in sight. The police officer at the information desk stood up and said, "It's the end of my shift. We're closing down for the night. You sure you're okay?"

"I'll nap here for the hour," I said with a tone not unlike a child ready to throw a temper tantrum.

"Rough start to your vacation, eh?"

Vacation. I thought about that word. I'd only been twenty-four hours without a home. Now my home was in the world. I was officially a nomad.

"No, I'm going home," I said.

Looking at me with surprise, he asked, "You live in Peru?"

I looked down at my blue sparkly sneakers. "Yes, you could say that. I live here," I said with shaky confidence as he waved goodnight.

I guess this is what beginning again feels like, I thought to myself. You make your home inside yourself.

I scanned the empty airport hall. I knew how to be me in my job and with my friends and family. But being out in the world—without a job, without people who knew me—felt like a tragic ending. If this was what new beginnings felt like, I wanted nothing to do with them.

GRIEF AS A PORTAL TO CHANGE

I've titled this chapter, "Can You Trust Yourself?" The simple answer is, yes, sister—you can absolutely trust yourself. Here's the surprising truth: I've found the more that women sit in their negative emotions, the more they can trust themselves in all areas of life. Why? Because a requirement of trusting yourself is developing a loving, ongoing relationship with grief. *Yes, you heard me correctly*. Just like you maintain a relationship with your mother-in-law or next-door neighbor (whether you actually like them or not), it works the same way with emotions (especially the negative ones). Developing a healthy relationship with your own cocktail of grief is the work of Soulcation, and the portal to true life change.

Grief is a feeling most of us would rather avoid. It's one that can take many forms, but it is most connected to six core elements:

1. Something ending
2. Something being outside our control
3. Losing something we love
4. Losing something we worked hard on or for
5. Disappointment
6. Unfulfilled goals, hopes, or desires

To cultivate a relationship with your grief, you first must acknowledge grief and bereavement are not the same. Bereavement is a period of intense suffering or mourning following the death of a loved one. Grief is a much more universal state of deep sadness that is not reserved for funerals. Although grief is certainly one reaction to major loss (and one I have profound compassion for and know personally because of my mother's death), it is not isolated to traumatic endings. In order to Soulcation, you need to see grief for what it truly is—an everyday, normal, common emotion. Humans are vessels for hope. It feels good to hope for the things you want. But on the other side of the act of hoping can come disappointment and grief for the unattained. Hope and grief are two sides of the same coin. When you ignore either side, you become emotionally unsatisfied, anxious, and unfulfilled. And while it's possible to ignore your hope, I find it's much more common for people to ignore their grief.

When we're not aware of or connected to our grief, it becomes invisible, and it often manifests as anger. In the state of experiencing invisible grief, we might experience anger at our boss for blocking our career goals, rage at our partner for not supporting our dreams, or have an outburst at the guy in line at the grocery store for taking too long at the checkout. We feel angry we can't have what we want on the timeline we had in mind. Sometimes we even feel anger and don't know the reason. We are *just* angry, and we will blow our fiery steam on anyone in range.

But if we slow down and get still within ourselves, we find that underneath anger is unprocessed grief. Just as author Claire Bidwell Smith writes in her book, *Anxiety: The Missing Stage of Grief*, "I sat with my anger long enough, until she told me her real name was grief."[7] Grief is hidden in most corners of our lives, and it's the bravest among us who say yes to feeling it.

Grief is normal. It is a critical part of fully living, and the medicine we need to change and grow as humans. In fact, there is a large body of research on "core emotions" that consistently classifies grief as one of the central human emotions. Along with grief, these core emotions typically include anger, sadness, joy, fear, and creative/sexual energy. Neurologically speaking, a core emotion is simply a frequent neurological signal that fires inside our nervous system, whether we consciously realize it is happening or not. We all regularly experience the body's signal that there is something to grieve. The tragedy of the modern world is that our everyday grief is too often dismissed, or worse, the ones who acknowledge it are labeled as "broken."

Imagine you're at a cocktail party and someone asks, "How are you doing?" You answer back, "I'm grieving right now. It's pretty hard." Perhaps just reading this sentence horrifies you and makes you feel like you committed a social faux pas. We give grief a place in our culture after a death or life-changing diagnosis, but we've done ourselves and our children an incredible disservice by not creating space in our culture for the emotion of grief to be a common one in daily life. We acknowledge what I call "capital G" Griefs (such as death), but "lowercase g" griefs—less visible things like unrequited love or a disappointment—go unwitnessed or not fully processed.

David Kessler is a therapist well-known for developing the stages of grief: denial, anger, bargaining, depression, acceptance, and added recently, a sixth stage: finding meaning.[8] His ideas were primarily informed by research among cancer and terminally ill patients, individuals experiencing capital G Griefs. However, when we apply this framework to the broader experience of grief, the risk is our concept of grief can take on a goal-orientation: i.e., our goal is to reach the other side of grief as fast as possible, rather than develop the inner tools for self-soothing while *staying in your grief.*

I remember when sweet Susan handed me the printout of the stages of grief after my mom died and asked me which one I was in. "Susan," I said, "I have no idea. I feel them all at once. It's like I'm on a hamster wheel moving so quickly I can't even notice what I'm feeling."

She looked back at me with her soft, knowing eyes and said, "You can't heal if you don't grieve, Mel." Then she went on to explain feelings are simply neurons firing in our body. "If you let the grief move through you and take up all the space it needs, the firing lasts for approximately ninety seconds. That's all. Everything else is the story you create in your head around what the grief means."

No way. It's impossible all this pain is connected to a story in my head, I thought.

But her words resonated for me. I was finding every activity possible to avoid sitting in my grief. I didn't trust grief could be good for me. I told myself it was bad and that I couldn't be a whole, happy human while "in a steady relationship" with it. But by fighting against it with all my strength, I was really blocking it from moving through me, alchemizing, and dissipating. An emotional sensation that was meant to last ninety seconds felt like it might last ninety years. Looking back, this resistance to grief was arguably my biggest barrier to making the change I wanted in my life, and to feeling good again. I thought I was stuck in grief, but I was really stuck in the *story I had created* about grief.

Why do we do this?

Because the work of life change requires grieving old identities, habits, and ways of being. You must grieve things to change things. Without grief you can't …

- Go from a dysfunctional relationship to a safe, healthy, and loving one
- Go from one mediocre job to running your own dream business
- Go from living with one set of values to living by a new, richer, more aligned set of values
- Go from one way of spending your "free" time to claiming most of your time as your own
- Go from living in the same town you always have to living in a new city
- Go from busy to playing, resting, and doing something on your Happy List every day
- Start that new project, choose that new lifestyle, take that sabbatical, say yes to that invitation, explore a new spiritual path, or find a new set of friends that support you in a grand leap
- Let go of the script you've been living for your life, and rewrite it, rejig the terms, and create an entirely new path for yourself

Grief is your medicine. It's what gets you from A to Z. From the life you have now to the life you want to have. If you're having a "hot mess" moment on a cold tile floor like I did in the Lima airport, it's likely *not* because you aren't trying or working hard enough. And it doesn't mean *anything* is wrong. It's likely because grief is stuck in your body with no place to move. Your grief hasn't (yet) been noticed or named. You haven't (yet) cultivated an actual relationship with grief. Your grief is suppressed—and it's keeping your life stagnant when you so badly want it to change.

The implications of dismissed or diminished grief are massive. It's the Achilles heel of life change and self-trust. Sister, if you have that feeling you're not where you want to be yet, it's likely because grief is hiding in the undercurrents of your life, begging to be witnessed. Your grief doesn't need fixing—it needs feeling. Like a good date, it needs you to take it out to dinner, sit attentively, ask questions, listen, and then snuggle up for a good make-out session and some foreplay to soak in all the feels. Because the part of ourselves that experiences unprocessed grief just wants us to make space and time for it to be witnessed and seen.

It is in this relationship with grief that we can explore questions such as:

- "What is the voice of ME?" as opposed to "What is the voice I was conditioned to hear but that may not actually be ME?"
- Where did I go to receive love, safety, and belonging as a child ... and are those ways still serving me?
- Where did I learn to abandon myself for the sake of feeling like I fit into my family as a child, and what parts of myself do I need to let die to finally step forward and unearth the REAL ME?

This is the work of Soulcation. We must grieve who we thought we were to be reborn into a more authentic version of ourselves: the self that existed before our families and the world told us who we *should be*. To do this you first need to pay attention to the soft whispers and nudges that feel like grief. Then, observe the stories you play on repeat in your head around the emotional sensations of grief. And finally, consider whether the story disappeared or was no longer true. You will likely find you're able to let yourself feel it and still be okay.

At first, grief will sting and hurt and feel like the end of the world (because in some ways it is the end of the mental construct of the world you've been living in). You will feel broken, heavy, and consumed with unfamiliar sensations. You will want to craft a story (typically with you as either a victim or villain) to make sense of the grief. You will want to pay whatever money you have to book a one-way ticket back to comfort land. But grief is normal. It asks us for space and attention, which once given, allows us to be in a healthy relationship with grief. It wants to work for us, not against us. When we let grief be our friend, we wake up one day and realize we can trust it, and when we can trust our negative feelings along with our positive ones, that's when we know we can really trust ourselves.

MAYBE IT WAS ALL A MISTAKE

I woke up groggy in my new Lima apartment and sank down on the red leather couch. Sun and ocean air flowed through the open bay windows, and a large Peruvian grandma wearing a wide-brimmed red hat and floral dress, washed clothes on the rooftop across the street. We made eye contact, clearly both curious about the seemingly foreign life of the other.

I had survived the travel day from hell. The clock showed 1:00 p.m. on Monday. I hadn't woken up this late since college. I sat there and stared at my phone, unsure what to do with my empty calendar, empty inbox, and empty heart. *Would I enjoy the blank canvas of this sabbatical? Could I actually write the book I want-*

ed? What if I was bad at it? Would I have fun or make friends in this town?

My phone buzzed with a familiar ping. It was a new email. I felt the dopamine rush I had become so addicted to back at the Gates Foundation. It was from a world-class, influential organization—one I had always dreamed of working for "someday." The title of the email was "available to chat Friday?" and inside was a short, cryptic note.

> Mel,
> I hope you are doing well. You came to my mind today. We have a leadership role open and I'd love to chat with you about it. When are you free?
> Signed,
> DB

When am I free?

I wanted to walk the beach and eat fresh Peruvian ceviche. There was also a fruit shop that made homemade popsicles I wanted to check out. But I could do that whenever. I looked down at my calendar. *When am I not free?* I looked up at the woman on the rooftop, who was now humming and swaying as if doing laundry brought her the greatest pleasure in the world. *Was she actually delighting in something as mundane as laundry*? I mentally filed this away under #lifegoal.

Two days later, I was on a Skype call with DB—he in his executive office, and me on my red couch in Lima, Peru.

"How are you, Mel?" he asked, sipping coffee from a corporate branded mug.

"Good, good. Thanks for asking, DB. I just started my sabbatical. I'm taking a few months off to travel, rest, play. You know ... have some fun. I'm in Lima, Peru now, doing, well, not much of anything yet."

He leaned back in his chair with a stoic face, as if the words "not doing much" needed extra time to process.

Oh shoot, oh shoot, oh shoot. I just said the wrong thing. If this is a job interview, I'm doing a terrible job showing I'm a responsible, hard worker.

He changed the subject.

"Well, Mel, we've been thinking about the future of the organization. We see a place for you here," he said, leaning back, crossing his arms, and launching into describing the dream job I had wanted for years. The organization. The title. The salary. Everything about it was perfect—or at least the version of perfect I had crafted in my head as the Gates Foundation version of Mel.

I could see myself there already, a senior executive living as an expat in Africa. I would rent a quiet house with a big backyard, a pool, and as many orange and mango trees as I wanted.

Could this dream still be mine for the taking? I did a little happy dance in my mind, shocked that the job I had worked so hard for—and thought would take years more to earn a seat at the leadership table—could be mine for the taking now.

"Wow, what a great offer, DB," I said. "This feels like it would be a perfect fit. Give me a few days to think about it, and DB, I'm glad you called. I'm really grateful for this opportunity."

I clicked my camera off and let the traffic outside fill the silence.

For months I'd been resisting the dark emotional tunnels in my life. It didn't seem fair, or possible, for something I've always wanted to come so easily, without any effort from me. I gazed out the window back to the woman in the red hat now hanging clothes on the line. I felt this urge to talk to her as if she were MY mom.

Mom, I just want you to tell me what to do! I screamed in my head.

My screams fell into the void, a reminder I couldn't turn to the people I once loved to make my life decisions anymore. So I pulled out my notebook and wrote "dream job" at the top of the page and drew a line down the middle. Under the "pros" column I listed: promotion, excellent pay, first management role, excellent vacation benefits, a country I love, an organization I love, good reputation, good boss. Then I wrote the finale: "Prove a divorced woman can be a strong woman. She can move to Africa alone. She can get promoted and kick ass even when the shit hits the fan." I looked down and smiled at this. Damn, it felt good. It could be my post-divorce victory play that would leave people with no question I could be served lemons and find a way to make lemonade.

Then the word "prove" hit me. I circled it on the page. *What was I trying to prove? And to whom exactly?* The truth was I had no idea. Next, I looked at the blank column labeled "cons." I couldn't think of one con. Literally, not even one. Accepting this offer felt like it could be my fast pass back to stability. *When you can't come up with anything negative, you've got your answer, Mel*, I thought. Then an idea hit me. I turned the page and wrote "dream life" at the top (instead of "dream job"). I already paid for this apartment in Peru for the next month, and I had plans to go to Spain to walk the five hundred-kilometer Camino de Santiago pilgrimage the following month. These were things on my Happy List—but they also were chock-full of the unknown. *I could have the time of my life, or I could get kidnapped and shuffled into the underground sex trade*, I thought. It was possible. Still, something in me started rattling off dreams and places and things I could do if I stuck with my sabbatical plan. Ideas came at lightning speed.

- Visit the English countryside
- Float in the Dead Sea and tour around Israel
- Start writing for real again, and maybe even write a book
- Learn to meditate
- Sign up for a yoga retreat
- Visit Paris and eat chocolate croissants for breakfast every day
- Sleep in without setting an alarm
- Start a blog
- Live off the grid and in nature somewhere in the jungle
- Find the cheapest, most isolated beaches in the world and relax
- Study bamboo architecture, and maybe live in a treehouse
- Go on a shopping spree in Italy
- Take a course in entrepreneurship

I stepped back and looked at the full page of dreams—wild, playful, downright crazy, *and expensive. Who am I to galivant away from everything I worked so hard for, to eat croissants and float on a plastic unicorn on a beach somewhere?* Plus, this list would exhaust my entire life savings ... and I still probably couldn't do it all. *Then what?* I would have a long stretch of "unicorn-floating unemployment" on my resume to explain to DB, or whoever else was sympathetic enough to meet with me when the time came.

I would be so dang good in this leadership role DB was offering. I didn't know if I would be good at—let alone like—traveling solo around the world. I didn't know how I would do at creative work: writing, blogging, and sharing my thoughts online. I didn't know if I'd find friends, or if I'd still feel like I was living in a lonely dark cave (even if that cave included dietary options of unlimited cheese and croissants). I didn't even know if this list was a reflection of the true Mel or just a crazy, indulgent Mel itching to hack her way out of feeling lousy as quickly as possible. That's when I heard my mom's voice, so clear it was like she was alive and with me: "Safety first, Mel. Safety first." I had wanted someone to tell me what to do for months now, and there in Lima, Peru I had finally received the download I'd needed from my deceased mom. *What could be clearer?*

But something in me paused. *Look where safety has gotten you,* I thought. *Certainly not to any state of bliss. Maybe there's another way?* It was time to reckon with the question I had been avoiding up until now. Was I going to be "good" or was I going to be wild and free?

THE ALCHEMY OF GRIEF

It was 6:00 a.m., and I slathered my feet in anti-blister cream, pulled on toe socks, and added the final layer: smart wool socks. I had a backpack full of water, sunscreen, and more blister cream than a human could ever need. It was my first time in Portugal, and I was wide-eyed and squeamish. I stood at the foot of the Porto Cathedral, gazing up in awe at the stone columns around a turquoise wood door, the burst of color bringing new life into a setting that screamed "ancient." There were candles burning on the altar outside, and the smell of incense filled the courtyard. I arrived early out of both caution and fear, with the intention to walk the day's twenty kilometers before the sun got unbearable.

I was at the starting point of the Portuguese Route of the Camino de Santiago: a spiritual pilgrimage from Porto, Portugal to Santiago, Spain. It was the path everyday seekers and spiritual gurus alike had walked for thousands of years. From what I read, the path traversed small villages, mountainous terrain, coastal flatlands, and some big towns en route to Santiago, where John, the apostle of Jesus, was buried, and a grandiose cathedral awaited. But I wasn't here for the cathedrals. I had taken Susan's advice. I was here to alchemize my grief through walking. My relationship with grief was in its infant stages, and I'd resonated with her suggestion that moving the physical body (she called it "moving mediation") was a proven way to process stuck emotions. It seemed like the most pleasurable route through the dark emotional tunnel, all while wrapped in a package that felt somewhat like a vacation. So here I was. I had left Lima and traveled across the world to Portugal to put one foot in front of the other until I had full access to the intensity of grief still stuck in my body.

I pointed my iPhone towards the cathedral and snapped a picture. Then I scanned the courtyard looking for the first yellow arrow. In all my research preparing for the hike, there were no maps guiding the way. There were only spray-painted yellow arrows—that apparently have existed for years—to mark the path. *Ha, that's impossible,* I thought. *How in the world will I traverse five hundred kilometers from one country to another relying on nothing but spray-painted arrows that God knows some smartass kid might switch in the middle of the night?*

"It's over there ..." an old man in a white priestly robe said as he walked by. I followed his finger to the steps past the courtyard. Then I looked back at his kind, wrinkly face.

"Trust the yellow arrow, miss. It will take you all the way home," he whispered into the dewy morning air. I smiled a doubtful smile. I was used to trusting Google maps, not arrows spray-painted on random walls, bricks, or stones. And trusting myself to notice each one of them was foreign territory.

As Mr. Priest Man walked toward the cathedral door, I headed to where he had pointed. On the ground beneath my feet, I saw it: the first yellow arrow. An electric tingling shot through my body. It was the only one I truly needed, but the anxiety of not knowing the next turn or the one after that still had me in "yellow arrow freak-out mode." *Why did I choose a vacation that was becoming a game of GPS whack-a-mole*? I was here to heal my anxiety, but so far it was only escalating with the stress of not knowing where I would turn next.

Then I noticed a stack of papers on a bench that read "Poem for the new Pilgrim, by Antonio Machado."

Traveler, your footprints
are the only road, nothing else.
Traveler, there is no road;
you make your own path as you walk.
As you walk, you make your own road,
and when you look back
you see the path
you will never travel again.
Traveler, there is no road;
only a ship's wake on the sea.

There is no road. You make your own path as you walk.

I let these words sink in. I still felt like I was in a dark, endless tunnel, weighed down by grief and unable to find my way. I needed a plan, an escape route, and perhaps even an IV with some more happy juice. Making my way by walking felt like poison—not medicine.

But here I was. At the beginning of the most mundane way I had ever spent time. I had signed up to follow thousands of yellow arrows, and I was full-on skeptical that this whole walking thing had anything to do with spiritual transformation. But the invitation before me was to either walk out my grief or take a cab to my stopping point and keep the secret to myself until my dying day. Good Girl Mel knew she only had one option.

I set out. As I left the cathedral, I spotted the next yellow arrow on an innocuous, four-foot-long rock on the ground. Then the next was on a ten-foot-high stone wall of someone's home. The yellow arrows took me through side streets of Porto, then onto a dirt path along the water. The arrows pointed me to cross a bridge over a stream. Then a mile later they pointed toward another bridge back to the other side of the stream. *These arrows are not following the most logical or efficient path, that's for sure.*

I put in my earbuds and started a podcast (because I was too annoyed to listen to my own voice). I walked past breathtaking lily fields, vast Portuguese vineyards, abandoned churches, and the occasional working water fountain where I could refill my CamelBak. Occasionally, I would see another human with a shell dangling from their backpack, the symbol for "pilgrim"). We would nod, say "Buen Camino!" (or "Blessings on your Camino" in English), and continue on.

Day after day I did this. I developed a routine, stopping each morning in some village—ideally with entertaining old men smoking cigars and playing cards—to "sip an espresso" and be on my way. I didn't know anyone. I didn't know where the next turn would be. I didn't know who I would meet that night, where I would sleep, or—let's be honest—what direction was north. It felt like my own version of the Oregon trail, but with Spanish wine at night. I was a Wanderer. Walker. Pilgrim. My days were unplanned. My steps were unpredictable. My calendar was blank. Step after step, day after day, thought after thought, I would go wherever the next yellow arrow sent me. *I was making my way by walking. And for the first time in my life, I was spending time with myself.*

You know what happened? I transformed.

I don't have adequate words for this, because on the outside it looked so mundane, so earthy, and so not the Zen or spiritual way of healing I thought I'd need to go through to heal my anxiety. I just walked. I thought about the blisters on my feet. I stared aimlessly out into the distance. I took delight in an espresso like it was the best thing that ever happened to me. And I scanned nature for the next yellow arrow. Each day I did this, my mind seemed a bit quieter, stiller, and less in control of me. I could sense I was slowly closing the eighteen-inch gap (that felt like eighteen million miles) between my head and my heart. And I felt like I was waking up to *feeling in my body (not just in my head)* again.

I became aware of how my mind would sizzle and spark throughout the day to control the future. I felt tingling in my toes and legs that went up into my arms. I started to wonder if this was my body's way of awakening to deeper layers of my grief. I felt heat pulsing on the surface of my skin, and recognized anger rising. I felt tightness in my hips and intense vibrations through my joints, sensations of pain for all I had lost. I knew all these sensations weren't only physical responses to the walking. The body was releasing something deeper. I was starting to feel my grief, not just think about it.

Little by little, step after step, day after day, it didn't look like much of anything. But it was a whole lot of *something*.

I was creating space for emotions to bubble to the surface and move around. The grief I had stored deep inside for decades was slowly finding a way out of the cracks of my heart. It was oozing into the blood rushing through my veins and the oxygen surrounding me in nature. The sensations were not just about the body. The alchemy of grief was beginning. I was feeling again—and the medicine of movement to connect with my feelings felt good.

CHAPTER 8: CLEAR SPACE

"This is the first, wildest, and wisest thing I know, that the soul exists and that it is built entirely out of attentiveness."

—Mary Oliver

I was at the yoga studio two blocks from my house. It had been a full week since that terrible-horrible-no-good-very-bad day when Brock blindsided me with his news of divorce. This class was the first time I had left the house since. The fact that my feet were planted on the mat felt nothing short of a miracle. As the instructor guided us in her soft, Zen voice, I awkwardly shifted my weight back and forth in downward dog, incapable of stillness. I thought yoga would be a good idea, but my body felt like a semitruck that was unmovable, stalled, and loaded with freight I felt pretty certain wouldn't be arriving at its destination. *What had I been thinking?*

For years I had heard teachers say, "If anything really doesn't feel good, just return to child's pose. It's always here for you." However, I never wanted to be *that* girl. You know, the kind who succumbed to her hands and knees while everyone else was "flipping their dog" like a badass yogi. Even in my week of rock bottom, I resisted—too proud to give myself the rest I desperately needed. I wiggled and squirmed and tolerated a full hour of discomfort waiting for the reward at the end: Savasana.

If you don't know what Savasana, or corpse pose, is let me introduce you to the very best thing in the whole wide world. It's technically called a "pose" (more on that later) but it's pretty much a glorious nap that you get permission to take at the end of class (which in my mind always made the $12.99 class fee worth it). The instructor guides you to stretch your feet out on the mat, palms up, eyes closed (as if any human really needs instruction to rest). Then they leave you there in silence to do ... drum roll please ... NOTHING. It's a glorious, peaceful ten minutes in silence.

For years, Savasana was arguably one of the only times I felt true rest. Inside the four walls of the yoga studio, I would let myself calm down, steady my breath, go inward, and yes, be still. I had been in the same yoga studio room for a few years, and each time we came to Savasana, I felt like I had found the proverbial pot of gold. I would bask in the feeling of ease and rest. Then—just as rainbows do—it would end, the time would be up, the feeling would disappear, and I'd go back to trying to manage the busyness that was my life.

Yet on this first class as a divorcee, as the instructor guided us into the delicious rest of Savasana, I had a thought: What if life could actually feel like Savasana? What if I could feel peace, stillness, and a sense of rest going about my ordinary, everyday life? What if Savasana wasn't just a pose I could bask in for two songs at the end of my hipster Seattle yoga class, but a way of life?

I wanted to stay in Savasana forever. It was the only thing that felt good in my shitstorm of a life. I just didn't yet know how to hold onto the feeling I got from the still moments on my yoga mat.

SAVASANA MUST BE LEARNED

Let me tell you something your mother likely didn't say enough. You can live a life that feels luxuriously restful, slow, and spacious.

Seriously, sister. It's possible. You have the power to make the changes, take back your time, and design a life full of all the prone body, palms-up naps you want. It may sound as crazy as me "flipping my dog" the week after my husband left, but stay with me. I've written this book to show you how. The trick is to approach the journey like you would learning a new language.

Rest is a skill.
And rest must be learned.

Learning to rest is a gradual process, but if you believe these two facts, you can design a life you don't need a vacation from. In Hindu tradition (where yoga originates) Savasana is considered the most challenging pose of all. It's not supposed to come easily. It's something one hones over an entire lifetime. All the other yoga poses are intended to condition the mind to slow and still, so you are clearer, more present, and ready for the grand finale of poses: Savasana. The physical pose is easy. But the art of sinking into complete stillness and awareness of the present moment is the work of our lives. As the scholar Thomas Merton writes in *Conjectures of a Guilty Bystander,* the world is constantly pulling us away from Savasana:

> *There is a pervasive form of contemporary violence to which the idealist most easily succumbs: activism and overwork. The rush and pressure of modern life are a form, perhaps the most common form, of its innate violence. To allow oneself to be carried away by a multitude of conflicting concerns, to surrender to too many demands, to commit oneself to too many projects, to want*

to help everyone in everything, is to succumb to violence. The frenzy of our activism neutralizes our work for peace. It destroys our own inner capacity for peace. It destroys the fruitfulness of our own work, because it kills the root of inner wisdom which makes work fruitful.[9]

Doing is the disease of modern society. And Savasana—or the art of intentional rest—is the pathway back to physical and mental homeostasis. Savasana is such a healing form of rest because it demands simultaneous slowing and surrender of both our *minds* and *bodies*. This is where so many of us miss out on the transformational medicine of rest. Our bodies may be in the resting position (lying on the couch watching Netflix or in a hammock reading) but our minds are still racing, worrying, or planning something in the future. Alternatively, our minds can be in a rested state (we are chopping vegetables or pulling weeds in the garden and our minds feel still) but our bodies are still moving, active, and holding tension. It is rare that both our minds and bodies are simultaneously in a state of rest.

This mind-body rest is the goal of Savasana, and quite frankly, of life. When we don't feel physically, mentally, or emotionally safe inside ourselves, it's impossible to achieve this state that I call *embodied rest*. Embodiment is about accessing the intelligence we hold in our bodies. If we are disconnected from ourselves then we cannot experience embodiment. That's why we need embodied rest. It's the one reliable pathway back home to ourselves, and ultimately to our joy.

Embodied rest isn't possible without turning toward our pain (more on that in Chapter 9). And embodied rest doesn't just one day happen to us. True, restorative, embodied, Savasana-esque rest must be practiced, honed, and cultivated. We can't just block time on our calendar and—voila!—have access to all the good feels. It must be learned. And to learn anything in life, there is an essential ingredient you must have: spaciousness. Spaciousness is the bridge that supports you on your journey out of what Thomas Merton describes as the self-violence of "activism and overwork" into an embodied, restful state of being.

If you imagine your life as a car cruising along at sixty-seven miles per hour in the fast lane, you're not going to be able to immediately shift to living life at five miles per hour. It's simply not possible. An off-ramp, deceleration, and down-shifting process is needed, right? Sure, you could try slamming on the brakes, but at best that's going to hurt and at the worst it could create a fifty-car pile-up. In order to Soulcation, the trick is to create physical, mental, and emotional space.

CREATE PHYSICAL SPACE

Soulcation is about falling back in love with your life. To do this, you need buffer, margin, and spaciousness in your days. According to Ayurveda, one of the world's oldest holistic healing systems developed in India, space is defined as absence or nothingness. The principle of spaciousness is based on the idea that *to know spaciousness you can't chase it; you must sit still and be receptive.* In essence, the work of creating space is the work of creating receptivity.

When I work one-on-one with clients, we always start with an assessment of physical space. Physical space includes two components: time and environment. These are the easiest dimensions to take immediate action on and thus see immediate results. This is because without actual physical space, there is no healing. Let me say that again. Without carving out physical space for YOU, there can be no healing. The good news is, if you do the work to create physical space for yourself, it has a ripple effect to more mental and emotional space as well.

Step #1: Create Space in Your Calendar

If your calendar is anything like mine was back when I worked at the Gates Foundation, there isn't much breathing room. There is blue block after blue block of meetings and tasks. The calendar squares color your day from sun-up to sun-down without *any breaks*. Sound familiar?

Let's do a quick inquiry into your calendar to take stock of the problem:

- Do you ever struggle to find time between meetings to eat lunch or go to the bathroom?
- Can you go all day without even checking in with your body, moving your body, or, heaven forbid, letting your body nap IN. THE. MIDDLE. OF. THE. DAY???
- Do you wait until the end of the day or when your to-do list is completed to take a break?
- Do you frequently work for hours straight without even getting up or stretching?
- Do you agree to squeeze in extra appointments in the afternoon or evening that bleed into your time to exercise, cook a nutritious meal, or have time to yourself?
- Are you so tired at the end of the day that you frequently collapse on the sofa and tell your kids you feel "brain-dead?"

If you answered yes to one or more of these questions, it's likely you need more physical space in your calendar. This is where I get tough on my clients. Soulcation won't work if you have a million and one priorities and say yes to a million and one meetings, or if you are okay with a Google calendar of back-to-back colored squares. As Thomas Merton said, "to surrender to too many demands, to commit oneself to too many projects, to want to help everyone in everything, is to succumb to violence."

To take back your physical space is an act of social and spiritual rebellion. As my friend Shelley Paxton, author of *Soulbbatical: A Corporate Rebel's Guide to Finding Your Best Life*, always reminds me, usually those who arrive at a life they love are rebel souls in one shape or size. So how do you rebel against the calendar monsters? You do it by channeling the same energy that has helped you be so efficient and get so much done, and you put it toward scheduling in "white space" with the same boss-lady gusto you schedule everything else.

Soulcation Planning Pro Tip:
Schedule white space like you schedule meetings with your boss.

We all need physical space to process what's happening in our day, check in with ourselves, and follow a new possibility or idea that unexpectedly emerges. It's these "appointments with ourselves" that help us go from *executing the day* to *living fully in charge of the day*. When I'm helping a client make this transition, I send them the Calendar Inventory Checklist. They are often skeptical at first. After all, most of my clients are successful professionals who clearly have solid skills in time management.

However, they most often have viewed their time through a lens of what they need to achieve, not how they can optimize for doing less, taking naps, taking rest breaks or, heaven forbid, having a middle-of-the-day orgasm.

Calendar Inventory Checklist

- What appointments or meetings am I going to that I don't want to?
- What appointments or meetings bring me energy?
- What appointments or meetings could I reduce the cadence of or cancel completely?
- Do I have breaks scheduled into my calendar system each day? If not, why?
- Where can I build in breaks (and put them in my calendar as actual, non-negotiable appointments)?

I once was at a Gates Foundation event with a very famous CEO. He gave a talk on leadership, and I'll never forget when he said something like, "My job as a leader is to spend most of my day thinking." Here he was, someone who achieved a rare level of world-changing influence and wealth, and his advice to us was to block most of our work hours for white space to simply *think*. This felt rebellious. And this rebel part of him clearly had a significant role in his success. While all his competitors and peers operated from a *doing mode*, he operated from a *slow and quiet thinking mode*. Similarly, Bill Gates is known for taking a "think week" every year. He goes to a small island, turns off his phone (yes, for the entire week), reads stacks of books, and goes on "thinking walks." Both these leaders practiced the skill of creating space.

It's not just leaders who need physical space. It's a core human need for everyone. I've written most of this book in lockdown. The world has lost many lives to COVID-19, and it's no doubt the biggest tragedy of our generation. But for those of us fortunate enough to have worked from home, I also believe the pandemic has been a powerful teacher of how to take back control of our calendars. We have discovered that achieving our goals doesn't necessarily require an exact eight hours a day slouching in front of a computer. We can be on email less, think more, and still get that promotion. We can take mid-day naps from home and still get everything done (and get it done with more ease and pleasure). We can take breaks, do some house chores between calls, and integrate our lives into our workdays. We can have more time to *think about work* (not just do it), and companies are better for it. Whatever change you made with your time during COVID-19, I think as a collective we are reckoning with the universal longing to slow down and create space. Our quality of life, and leadership, arguably depend on it.

Step #2: Create a "Soulcation" Environment

The second step to creating physical space revolves around intentionally designing your environment. To those who are highly production-oriented or feel strapped for time, what I'm about to say may seem extravagant, frivolous, or just not your jam. "*I'm fine with my white walls, thank you very much Mel,*" you're thinking. However, at a subconscious level, the space around us serves as a subtle reflection of our inner beliefs about ourselves. If you haven't yet decorated your home office or you're too lazy to hang that art you love in the hall, you're fundamentally saying to yourself, "I'm not worthy of beauty around me." You want space and beauty to be convenient, but at its essence, beauty is a thoughtful, slow, and creative effort. Thus, to reverse the belief that you are unworthy of a spacious life, you need to make choices that evoke feelings of beauty, restfulness, and spaciousness in the places you occupy most each day.

Let me pause here and say it's okay if you don't (yet) enjoy the space in which you live. I didn't for years. I was traveling for work so much that when I was home the last thing I wanted to do was put effort into home projects. It was "frivolous and a waste of money," I told myself. So, I tolerated a home with poorly built IKEA furniture, no interior design, and not much character. I enjoyed beautiful spaces when I went on vacation, not at home. However, beauty, my friend, is a powerful way to create a feeling of spaciousness in your life. When you start curating things you *really* love and that *really* bring you joy in your home or office, it brings a sense of ease. It becomes easier to pause, slow down, and be in the present moment because you enjoy your present space. The good news is, this can all be done in baby steps, spread out over time.

You don't need to redecorate the entire house. But maybe you give yourself a budget to add one thing that evokes beauty each month. Or maybe you start a Pinterest board of images and places that inspire beauty. My friend Kelly created a Soulcation environment by adding a writing desk in her bedroom. Another friend created a Soulcation environment by scheduling an appointment for West Elm to come and give her design tips for how to move the furniture around in her home (for free, by the way). Another client created her Soulcation environment by color coding her bookshelf, and another by getting a handcrafted bedside table that could fit the oils, journal, and meditation pillow she used to support her morning routine each day. Once I left the Gates Foundation and was on sabbatical without a home, I created a Soulcation environment by renting Airbnbs in different cities with tasteful interior design. I would save my favorites, and then go back through the list of options, and as Marie Kondo teaches, ask myself, "Does this style and space bring me joy?" When the answer was yes, I would book.

Interior designers will tell you the effort and thought put into curating beautiful spaces is *so they can be enjoyed*. The catch is people can only enjoy them when they're *fully present*. This is the power of creating beauty in your space. It psychologically prompts you to slow down and enjoy what is around you, which is the essence of Soulcation. At its core, beauty is defined by the things that make your heart soften, slow, and draw towards love. I always tell my clients, "The soul knows what it loves. It doesn't need to be taught." Beauty forces us to be humans who enjoy and love. And enjoyment and love, sister, are the paths back home to ourselves.

If you want to feel more spaciousness in life, become a curator of beauty in your life. If you don't know where to start, use this checklist:

Soulcation Planning Pro Tip:
Create a Beauty Map

Beauty Inventory Checklist

- What places inspire you?
- What images on Pinterest inspire you?
- What Instagram accounts inspire you?
- What would make your home more beautiful?

- What space in your home could serve as your "Soulcation" space?
- What would connect you with beauty throughout the day?
- What could you gift yourself that would make you feel more beautiful?
- Where do you want to go to inspire beauty?
- What scents evoke stillness and calm in you?
- What colors and art are you drawn to?
- What architecture and design do you seek out on vacation? How could you bring this essence into your everyday life?

CREATE MENTAL SPACE

One day my good friend Sarah called me up and said, "Mel, I don't know what it is, but I feel so jumbly. My brain is like a ball of mush. I can't concentrate, I can't work, and my thoughts are ping-ponging around like a spiderweb."

While "jumbly" isn't a clinical diagnosis, we all know the feeling. Our minds buzz with all sorts of thoughts that despite our good effort, we can't seem to still. We feel trapped in our heads. Life is scattered. And our "jumbly-ness" keeps us everywhere and anywhere but fully present.

"Mel, I don't know what to do," Sarah said, defeated. "I'm trying to pull myself out of this, but I just keep overthinking."

Nearly every week, as we were both in major life transitions, Sarah and I would catch up on the phone about our respective jumbly feelings. We would recap and analyze the ways our minds had been on turbo mode overthinking that week. And while it helped to speak our thoughts out loud, as time went on, it became clear we couldn't heal our overthinking minds with more thinking. *How could we, once and for all, crawl out of life's jumbly-ness?* we wondered.

The answer is we needed to create mental space. For Soulcation, mental space is defined as daily rhythms of stillness, slowness, and rest that allow us to process the events of the day, connect with self, and notice the sensations, feelings, and objects in our present moment. Achieving mental space is at the core of mindfulness and the science of mindfulness-based stress reduction.

According to www.mindful.org, "mindfulness is the basic human ability to be fully present, aware of where we are and what we're doing, and not overly reactive or overwhelmed by what's going on around us."[10] This can only happen when we dedicate time and energy to letting our bodies process thoughts and feelings. This can be done through meditation, yoga, walking, short pauses in everyday life, or essentially anything that makes the mind feel quiet. As Rumi writes, "The quieter you become, the more you are able to hear." When we feel rushed is when we're most likely to avoid an emotional tunnel, create an untrue story about a feeling, or manipulate to get an outcome. But when we have the mental space to be with our thoughts and feelings without jumping to any outcome, we are set free.

Step #1: Take Radical Responsibility for Yourself

One of the biggest reasons people don't have enough mental space is they have subconsciously outsourced the work of feeling loved to others and use way too much mental energy trying to keep a steady supply coming in. The truth is love—and life—are inside jobs. We are the ones responsible for meeting our needs and cultivating love, beauty, and spaciousness in our lives. No one else can do it for us. No one is going to swoop in and magically gift you with mental space. The buck ultimately stops with you, sister.

Yet when we look outward for permission, love, or validation, it becomes a slippery slope, with the most immediate cost being taking up a shitload of mental space. You can have a manageable calendar and supportive physical space in your life but still feel chronically jumbly. This is because mental space requires taking radical responsibility for giving yourself the love you want from others. In his book, *Loveability: Knowing How to Love and Be Loved*, Robert Holden, PhD, describes it well. He writes that lack of mental space

> *"... arises when you feel unloveable and see others as your source of love. This causes you to enroll your mother, your partner, or your children, for instance, into making you feel more loveable. They may not know it, but they have a contract of employment. You believe it's their job to make you feel whole, secure, and connected to the world, to heal your wounds, and to validate you. Inevitably, though, when you make someone your source of love, they will also be a source of pain. No one does a very good job making someone feel loveable, mostly because it's an impossible task. People can encourage you to feel loveable, but they can't make you feel loveable. Making sure you feel loveable is your job, not someone else's."*[11]

The practice of self-love is a freedom practice. We practice it by taking full responsibility for cultivating love and joy in our lives. And the benefit is we set up our mind to be free from jumbly-ness.

Step #2: Get Clear on What Matters Most

The second reason we lack mental space is we aren't clear internally on what we want. We let our lives fill to the brim with things to do. All these things suck our mental energy until there is little left to even consider whether the things we do are the *right* or *most pleasurable* for us to be doing. We keep saying yes. It gives us a sense of forward momentum. But we also can't remember the last time we felt all sparkly and on fire for life.

The writer, musician, and entrepreneur Derek Sivers once wrote a blog post where he said, "If I'm not saying, 'HELL YEAH!' to something, then I say no."[12] Mark Manson went on to apply this principle to dating. And here inside the pages of Soulcation, I'm taking it one step further and applying it to the soul. I call this the Soulcation Equation. That is, if a person, situation, project, invitation, or activity does not inspire a "Fuck Yes" in you, then it is a "Hell No."

Before you get all logical on me, I get it. We still have to pay our taxes, wash the dishes, and scrub toilets sometimes. The Soulcation Equation is also subject to the 80/20 rule. But the entertainment you choose, the people you go to happy hours with, the calls you pick up, your career moves, the ways you spend your money, and where you live are all within your control. If you don't wake up each morning, pour your coffee, look at your calendar, and think, *fuck yes, this lights me up* then it's likely a "hell no." The point is: if you're not a "fuck yes" in your body and soul about something, the decision should easily be a "hell no." No mental gymnastics or jumbly spinning needed. If you're not sure, it's likely a no. (And yes, many of you might want to pause right here and send off a few politely worded "hell no" Soulcation texts.)

The "hell no" list can give the heebie-jeebies to people-pleasers who don't like conflict. I hear it all the time: "But Mel, I can't say no to THAT." Well, sister, I'm here to say YES. YOU. CAN. I'm not saying it won't be the fight of your life. I'm saying the Soulcation Equation of "Fuck Yes" and "Hell No" is the only way to set your soul free.

Soulcation Planning Pro Tip:
Make a Fuck Yes vs. Hell No List

Here is an example:

FUCK YES	HELL NO
• Morning writing practice • Interviewing interesting people on my podcast • Strategy work for my company • High-paid consulting gigs • Eating orgasmic meals • Weekly yoga and sound baths • Full moon parties	• Going out with Adam • Taking calls in the mornings • Consulting for companies that don't inspire me • Drinking • Texting a lot before going on a first date • Explaining my choices to old friends

CREATE EMOTIONAL SPACE

Step #1: Feel All Your Feelings

Far too many of us were never taught how to appropriately feel our feelings. Growing up, I learned negative emotions were a sign of weakness. I am a highly sensitive person by nature, so as you can imagine, hiding my grief, anger, and sadness only worked for so long. You can't think one way and feel another, then expect anything in your life to change. As we've discussed with emotional tunnels, when we refuse to create space for negative emotions, we block our body's natural process of releasing them, and this, soul sisters, is a root cause of stress and emotional illness. A good place to start getting curious about what negative emotions are stuck inside you is through this Emotional Inventory Checklist.

Emotional Inventory Checklist

- What feelings do you tend to feel most often?
- What feelings do you avoid expressing or block yourself from feeling?
- What feelings were you not taught how to feel?
- Who do you feel safe saying your feelings out loud to?
- What are the most frequent emotions you feel?
- How do they present themselves in your body?
- What negative emotion do you know you need to turn toward but have been avoiding?

Emotions control us when there is no space to let them breathe and dissipate. But when we create space for them, we turn the process around. We run our emotions, rather than letting them run us. After a lot of healing work, my friend Sarah (the same one with jumbly feelings) said to me recently, "Feeling is indeed the path to healing, Mel. To learn to rest is to learn how to feel. And to learn how to feel is to learn how to rest."

When you get into new territory with your emotions, I always tell my clients to think of it as a game. Your job is only to be exploring possibilities. You are likely not sure who your team members will be, what the plays will be, and whether you'll run or pass, fire your coach or keep them for life, or whether you'll need to do more strength training or cardio to move to the next level. You may not even know where you'll get your resources. You don't need to. All of that will unfold with time. Your job is to commit to showing up on the field and playing.

The art of clearing space for your soul to breathe is a lifetime sport. The key to being a good player is always to create enough time on your calendar, enough beauty around you, and enough awareness of your emotions that you feel supported to stay in the arena—playing and splashing around in the messy, earthy soil—rather than being a spectator on the sidelines of the game (and your life), wondering why everyone else on the field looks so damn happy.

CHOOSE YOURSELF

My body was trembling as I sat in front of the computer, staring at The Email. It had been weeks since I sent The Email to DB declining the job offer. I still came back to look over its content almost daily. I wondered how he interpreted each word, and most of all, I debated within myself whether I had made the right decision.

To calm my anxiety, I typed in "yoga retreat" into the Google search bar. *If I'm going to chase the feeling of Savasana, what better way than a yoga retreat, right?!* I spent three hours in a Google rabbit hole, browsing pictures of jungle-y yoga chalets, off the beaten path beaches, and women in bikinis who looked so freakin' happy doing yoga. I wondered if they were also happy when they went back home to their lives in the suburbs. Regardless, I was still ready to throw down good money for a week of green juice and Savasana. After all, what else did I have to do?

By the fourth hour of my internet binge I had a spreadsheet with prices, locations, and reviews. Then I landed on the website for Unsettled. It was a travel company who offered an "off-the-grid retreat." Their tagline was "Embrace the Unknown. Live Unsettled," and the page pitched it as a chance to completely exit society for a week. I would eat only food grown off the land, shower in harvested rainwater, and use electricity generated from solar panels. I would sleep when the sun went down and wake when it came up. No phone. No clock. No agenda. Yoga would be combined with food prep, cocoa ceremonies, and walks in the jungle on the protected land of Punta Mona in Costa Rica. I felt a spark in my body. *Yes, yes do that,* it said. And while it was still a few months away, the idea of leaving the busy world sounded divine. Savasana on steroids. I listened to my body and clicked purchase. And went to bed with a sense that there was more rest ahead.

CHAPTER 9: TURN TOWARD YOUR PAIN

"We try so hard to defeat the painful parts of ourselves, not realizing that's where the soul resides."

–Frances Weller

I sat in soft grass on the Tuscan hillside of San Gimignano. My view was filled with rolling vineyards and a smattering of old stone farmhouses. I inhaled a deep sense of gratitude for taking this leap. I had finished the Camino de Santiago and stayed in the region. And now I breathed in the scent of tomatoes fresh from the vine, along with onions and herbs from the kitchen, all part of life at a hundred-year-old family vineyard where meals together were a required affair.

Today I found myself in a circle of twelve strangers from all over the world, all staying at the vineyard for a week to devote ourselves to our shared interest in writing. Except for the emails, memos, and decks that had kept me busy at the Gates Foundation, I hadn't written a word in years. However, that day at the Willows Lodge I wrote "write a book" on my Happy List, and there was fire in my belly to see if I could.

I sat with a blank journal in front of me, and Darcie, the retreat leader, said, "We're going to do introductions a bit differently. You have five minutes to write down what you want people to know about you. No judgment. No over-thinking. Just write down what comes to mind."

Boom, I've got this, I thought, as my cool jobs, accomplishments, and unique places I had traveled all came to mind and flowed onto the page. When the timer buzzed, I stared down at my intro. *Heck, I AM interesting!* Next Darcie asked us to turn to a new blank page.

"All right, now for your second prompt. This time, I want you to write down what you DO NOT want people to know about you."

My heart skipped a beat. *Um, what?! How are all these people okay with this prompt*?

I wanted to escape all my secrets, not write about them. I scanned the room. Everyone else had already picked up their pens. My heart raced. I took a deep breath and began.

Tuscany, Italy: September 14, 2018

What I Don't Want People to Know About Me

> *I don't want people to know about my deep, chronic feeling of loneliness. Even with a big professional network and friends, most days I feel like my inner world is its own ignored island. I don't want people to know my husband recently divorced me and that the pastor at our church sat me down and pretty much told me it was my fault. Since that conversation, I've felt like I'll never be worthy of love again.*
>
> *I don't want people to know the secret that on the day my mom went into hospice, I was violent to my ex-husband.*

I don't want people to know about my anxiety attacks—all of them—but especially the one that landed me in the emergency room. I don't want people to know how much my mother's death still haunts me and how many weekends it kept me from getting out of bed.

I don't want people to know how much I was faking it—fawning and manipulating my way through my work. Keeping track of all my little white lies and not getting caught was exhausting. I don't want people to know how much I hate myself—my acne-prone skin, my nails I bite constantly, my big butt, and especially my vagina, which in my short time being married, my ex-husband refused to come down on. And to top it off, I don't want the people here—in Tuscany—to know that I'm not a real writer. In fact, I'm at a writing retreat and I haven't written a word in years. I'm a fake. An anxiety-ridden, emotional fireball of a woman (or let's be honest, girl) that is simply disguised as someone who has her shit together.

Whew!

I put my pen down and stared up at the horses grazing in the field beside our stone chateau. There it was. Everything I didn't want people to know.

"Okay, it's time to share," Darcie said, interrupting my thoughts. "We're going to take turns going around and reading what we wrote."

What in the world? This is a writing retreat, not a reading-out-loud retreat. How dare they make us read this out loud! I'm not prepared for this. My monkey mind went into high gear. *What excuse can I make to get out of this? Could I go to the bathroom and not come back? Or make something else up quickly enough to replace what I really wrote?*

Darcie made eye contact with me, and said, "Mel, why don't you go first?"

Palms sweating, I stared down at my journal. *Holy fuck, this is my worst nightmare come true.* Some people are all Brené Brown and intentionally lean into vulnerability like a spiritually woke human. But I was not that person, and all I could think was that the universe knew and was playing a cruel trick on me.

I took a deep breath, bit my lip, dipped my head down below the sightline of the other writers, and began to read. I tucked my legs under my body and felt my heart pulsing a mile a minute as I spoke. I wished everything on the page was not true, but it was. When I got to the final line—*"an anxiety-ridden, emotional fireball of a woman"*—I glanced up, certain I was about to die.

The group was dead silent—exactly like the dead feeling in my body. Darcie broke the silence, saying, "Thanks for sharing, Mel. That vulnerability was beautiful. You're clearly a natural. All right, now who's next?"

That's all? No sirens or guilt speech or Italian police marching over the hillside sentencing me with life in prison? Just, "Thanks ... next?"

I spent the next thirty minutes in my head, ignoring everyone else's introductions and coming up with an excuse for why I needed to get in a cab and leave immediately. I was shaken out of my mental escape planning when Darcie said, "Thanks everyone for sharing. Now that we've gotten to know each other, it's time for dinner." She pointed towards the long table under a pergola, already set with pitchers of wine, fresh caprese salad, and the most glorious cheese plate I had ever seen. *Boy, am I hungry.*

Before I could reach for the cab driver's number, a woman named Regina came up to me and said, "Mel, I know we just met, but can I give you a hug?"

I stood like a skyscraper as she reached in for a hug.

"I'm so sorry for what you've gone through. I've also been through a nasty divorce. It hurts like hell, and I had a similar reaction to yours." I stared at her blankly, still in shock that anyone would want to talk to me after meeting the dark and dangerous side of Mel. Then with her arms still on my shoulders she said, "Lean into this. If you turn toward your pain, it will set you free." Her words vibrated like a melody in my heart.

If you turn toward your pain, it will set you free.

If you turn toward your pain, it will set you free.

If you turn toward your pain, it will set you free.

Then she grabbed my hand—as if she knew I was about to flee—and walked with me toward the pergola. An old Italian grandpa handed me a slice of fresh parmesan. My mouth filled with cheesy delight, and for the first time in a long time, a wave of peace flooded my body. *Perhaps telling the truth doesn't always have to lead to a dark prison cell of judgment. Perhaps there is another way that these writer folks can teach me.*

THE TRUTH WILL SET YOU FREE

Accommodating and appeasing others' needs at the expense of our own is part of the disease of self-betrayal. We all know those people (and perhaps like me, you are one of them) living in what I call an anesthetized state of "fake calm." They pretend everything is fine on the outside because they so badly *want* to be a person with a calm persona. But locked away underneath is a simmering firestorm. It inevitably builds up like a cancer and sucks all the life out of the person. If you're friends with one of these people, you can usually see the train wreck coming before they can. But anesthesia only lasts so long. At some point, the unmet wants, needs, and desires inside of us unleash their fire, and the heat impacts everything and everyone in its path.

That day in Tuscany was the first time I publicly admitted to things I didn't want *anyone* to know about. I was a woman filled with untamed rage. And in all my work to make amends and understand my relationship with anger up until that point, I hadn't faced something critical to my freedom: my shame about all the rage that filled my body.

Guilt is defined as *doing* something wrong. Shame is a feeling of *being* wrong. Someone can forgive us for our actions, but it is usually the invisible undercurrent of shame—or the simmering rage that never quite reaches the surface—that eats us alive and keeps us stuck in life. Growing up in an extremely evangelical Christian culture, I inherited a lot of religious "rules": no sex before marriage, no dating around, no alcohol, get good grades, be polite and helpful, and even that a woman's role is to submit to a man's leadership. My mother groomed me to be this version of a "good girl." The God I was taught to follow had people going to Heaven and Hell, and my mind spent most of its energy trying to be on the winning side of this "good girl" calculation. However, the result of these beliefs was that I carried a whole lot of anger for having to always deny myself what felt good, and a whole lot of shame for my mistakes. My response to shame was to turn *outward* and *away*.

Outward toward people, projects, performance, and production, and away from my feelings, inner world, and very soul. I carried my secrets with me like a million-pound boulder and walked through the world scared to ever whisper the truth for fear people would remind me I wasn't who I wanted to be.

When we deny, dismiss, or ignore our pain, it haunts us. But when we name it, share it, and speak to it like a loving, compassionate mother, it begins to ease. Freeing your soul requires three things: (a) you turn toward your pain, (b) you make peace with your pain, and (c) you transform your pain into purpose. This is the whole point of a Soulcation: to create enough spaciousness and emotional safety to turn toward your pain. Because this *turning toward* is the most powerful medicine on the planet for a wounded soul. As Mary Oliver writes:

> *"You do not have to be good.*
> *You do not have to walk on your knees*
> *for a hundred miles through the desert repenting.*
> *You only have to let the soft animal of your body*
> *love what it loves.*
> *Tell me about despair, yours, and I will tell you mine.*
> *Meanwhile the world goes on.*
> *Meanwhile the sun and the clear pebbles of the rain*
> *are moving across the landscapes,*
> *over the prairies and the deep trees,*
> *the mountains and the rivers.*
> *Meanwhile the wild geese, high in the clean blue air,*
> *are heading home again.*
> *Whoever you are, no matter how lonely,*
> *the world offers itself to your imagination,*

calls to you like the wild geese, harsh and exciting -
over and over announcing your place
in the family of things."[13]

For me, turning toward my pain involved looking at my anger. Feeling anger is part of being human. It's one of the five core emotions. Yet when we stuff our anger down or push it away because we believe it is bad, rather than get curious about it, we live in bondage. As I look back on my own "good girl" patterns, the deeper problem was I didn't know how to listen to my anger. I was operating out of the unconscious programming that women were supposed to be calm, nice, kind, and not angry.

Control your emotions.

Stay quiet.

Don't get angry.

No one had ever taught me to get curious and listen to my anger. I didn't feel comfortable with anger. I sure as heck didn't think of it as a guide telling me where boundaries were crossed, where a need wasn't met, and where I was abandoning myself. But that's exactly what anger offers us. Anger is heat and fire. Anger can burn or it can illuminate. It can make gold or set our house on fire. Left unchecked, it can turn into rage, like it did in my case after years of living under the "good girl" complex. But when tenderly noticed, it can be a guide to show us where boundaries have been crossed, where we are out of alignment, and where we have unmet needs, desires, or feelings we need to tend to. Anger is a gift that shows us when we have drifted away from ourselves. There was a serious apology and a lot of shame after I hit my husband, and I wholeheartedly believe we should all be held accountable (and there should be consequences for our actions). But the goal is not to get rid of our anger, sisters. If we do that, we lose a key part of our internal GPS. The simmering has nowhere to release its steam—and we make our bodies and souls sick. Instead, the goal is to express and give appropriate voice to our anger. The goal is clean anger.

Clean anger is central to being a human.

Clean anger is a feeling you were meant to feel.

Clean anger is telling you a boundary has been crossed.

Clean anger is telling you something isn't right.

Clean anger is telling you that you have a valid, unmet need.

Clean anger is telling you to use your voice and speak a truth.

Clean anger is raising a red flag to recognize pain you need to turn toward.

Clean anger is telling you it's time to have that hard conversation.

Clean anger is your guide.

Clean anger is your friend.

Clean anger is even love.

Clean anger is on your side, simply asking you to be your own best lover and stop tolerating something that isn't okay.

It's important to note that anger—both dirty and clean—is not YOU. You are separate from your emotions. They are a part of you but they don't run the show. Think of it like a boardroom. Anger has a seat at the table. Anger is hanging around, and it's wise to turn toward it and give it a chance to speak. But you are still at the head of the table. You are in charge. You listen and can talk back to anger.

The magical thing is when you get quiet and curious and start listening to your anger, it really is quite loving. Let me explain. If you enter the tunnel of your anger, my hunch is you will find it's trying to look out for you. It's trying to warn you when something isn't okay or some person isn't safe. It's trying to prompt you to use your voice or reinforce a boundary or ask for something. Anger is trying to guide you back to your soul's truth. Anger doesn't ask you to walk a hundred miles on your knees through the desert to escape it. All it asks is that you turn *toward* it and heed its wisdom.

We are all stuck in our pain waiting for someone to go first and give us permission to do the same. I've gone first here, but now it's your turn.

Clean Anger Checklist

- What do you not want people to know about you?
- What anger do you need to turn toward?
- What is your anger saying to you about what boundaries have been crossed or needs that have been denied?

Give your anger voice. And let the truth set you free.

PAIN AS A PORTAL TO A NEW LIFE

The next stop on my sabbatical was Koh Lanta, Thailand. I found this tiny gem of a town from a Google search of "world's best beaches off the beaten path." (Everyone should Google this at least once a year, by the way.) It was ranked among the top ten in the world, and lucky for me, the digital nomad company Hacker Paradise was running a month-long retreat in this tiny town. I had heard of Hacker Paradise through a few "digital nomads" I met in Peru, and the concept of co-working and co-living made me feel sparks of hope through my lonely soul. It was a way to travel where I wanted and do it with friends. Well, technically strangers you paid money to become friends with as part of an organized retreat—but I fell for the sales pitch easily. After all, I was now on a mission to make my way down my Happy List, and doing it in community sounded way more fun than alone.

Koh Lanta is located on the southwestern tip of Thailand. The town had poorly paved roads, a smattering of tuk tuks, and roadside carts selling coconuts and pad thai for pennies. Bamboo huts had been turned into beach bars. Bed swings made from driftwood and handmade cushions served as chairs. The sand was white, the water was blue, and once I arrived, I felt transported to a place I thought only honeymooners or couples celebrating an anniversary were allowed to indulge in. That day in the bathtub at Willows Lodge, when I could barely come up for air, I had imagined myself living out my Happy List on a beach like this. Empty. Still. Peaceful.

The first day of the retreat kicked off in Koh Lanta's only co-working space. It was an outdoor garden oasis, with trees, hammocks, and private bungalows full of cushions you could use as call rooms. *People actually work here?* I wondered. The Gates Foundation offices, full of floor-to-ceiling glass, organic lunches, and unlimited Reese's Pieces had good perks, but this was next level. The orientation taught us how to use the facility's website to order a coconut straight to your desk.

"Massages are available here in the garden for $25 USD," Sara, the facilitator, went on to say.

We got all set up with high-speed Wi-Fi, paid our $100 membership fee, and spent the next hour introducing ourselves. There was Manoj, a tall, lanky guy who looked like a mixture of shaman and motorcyclist. Next to him sat Joe, a polished, bald Londoner whose British accent had me smitten at the first word. On the other side of the table were Beth and Jessie, both American freelancers who had been traveling the world for a while and seemed to know how to do this whole work remotely thing. And Tyler ... *oh Tyler*! He was the attractive jock type who rented his own tuk tuk for the month. Finally, there was Sara, a flirty Italian responsible for facilitating the trip and helping this group of fifteen global citizens survive alongside each other for a month. After warning us about the monkeys that could find their way into our rooms and eat our food if we didn't keep the doors closed, she handed us our room keys. I was in a new country with new people, but I fell asleep that first night thinking, *this feels like truly living.*

I settled into Koh Lanta easily. It was a small and simple town, nothing like the big city I left back in Seattle. I would walk the two-mile stretch of beach each morning, plug away at my writing practice during the day, and meet the Hacker Paradise crew at Lym's—our favorite bamboo shack beach bar—each night for sunset drinks, swims, and play time on Sara's group gift, an enormous floating unicorn we called Sparkles. Our days were simple. Our diet was mostly noodles and rice. Our life was lived mostly without shoes, in the sand. Life was quiet and slow, and extraordinarily good.

One night I took a tuk tuk to the other side of the island for some alone time. It was a few days before Valentine's Day, and I had started to feel that gnarly "single woman" panic that was rampant around this time each February. I was angry at Brock, God, my parents for letting me marry, and even the tuk tuk driver who took one wrong turn. I wanted red roses and a romantic beachside dinner, not abandonment or divorce or to have to pick up the pieces of my life in my thirties by myself. As I sat on my towel and got ready for sunset, I scanned the horizon. A married couple, wearing matching white linen, were holding hands and walking along the shore. She was beautiful. He looked strong and safe. Together, they looked happy, connected, and at peace. I felt the lust in my body and a burst of pleasure from vicariously living through their giggles and touches.

I'd fought so hard in my marriage to honor my wedding vows. I served, sacrificed, and provided for Brock. *But why hadn't I served and provided for myself with the same gusto?* I wondered. My body got unusually still as the sky filled with pinks and yellows. *Why did I stay in a painful marriage for so long? Why did I let pain become so normal? So familiar?* As much as I wanted a date for Valentine's Day, I wanted to know in my soul I wouldn't repeat the past even more.

That night I returned from the beach and sent a message to the entire Hacker Paradise group:

> *Y'all I need to burn some things. Like seriously light some old shit on fire. Who's down for a bonfire Friday night? I'm thinking wine, stars, and lots of big flames? Respond with the fire emoji if you're in...*

I went to bed. In the morning I woke up to a long thread of fire emojis. We picked the most isolated beach on the island without bars, electricity, or other people. When Friday came, Tyler arrived early and dug a fire pit in the sand, including "sand benches" for us to sit around. Manoj brought his ukulele. Joe and Sara brought boxes of wine, towels, and some paper and pens.

Hot-jock Tyler even acted as a spiritual shaman for the night, on a mission to make this passage sacred for me. "All right everyone, quiet down. We're here to light some shit on fire," he said with just the right mix of authority and humor. Manoj started plucking away at the ukulele.

"We are gathering tonight around this fire to name the pain we want to let go of. Mel has some things she wants to burn, but there are paper and pens here if you want to go as well."

My body tightened, and I felt a tingling from my fingers all the way down my legs. It took everything in me to stand up. I was wearing a black jumpsuit—reflective of the darkness in my soul. Red flames flickered over my face as I read the first piece of paper out loud.

"I let go of the belief that because my ex-husband doesn't love me, I'm not loveable," I said.

Then I walked to the fire and put my head over the logs, feeling the heat on my face. I held out the paper and watched as the tip caught on fire. I held onto it, letting the flames close in on my fingers. I waited until I was about to get burned, then—*Woooooosh!*—dropped it into the fire.

I took a deep breath.

I had seventeen things I wanted to let go of, including my lifelong dysfunctional relationship with anger, my identity as a divorcee, my habit of mimicking my mother's people-pleasing ways, and the belief I would always be lonely. I repeated the process of saying the hurt out loud, leaning over the flame, and letting the fire get all too close to my skin before releasing. The ukulele strummed. Our little rag-tag community stood by as witnesses. And the stars assumed their positions in the sky. Seventeen times I held my face over the flame, surrendering to its heat and energy. Currents of electricity rushed through my body. I was tangibly burning old parts of me, in the hope that the ashes emerging would birth new life in me.

Keep turning toward your pain, Mel; turn toward your pain, I kept saying to myself.

Tyler threw another log onto the fire. I pulled out a large sapphire ring tucked in my pocket. I bought it while passing through Bangkok at a jeweler well-known among expats. It was the most expensive piece of jewelry I had ever purchased. And I had a plan for it. I had been working on vows to myself—similar to wedding vows, but commitments to MYSELF instead. Promises for how I would love ME. Not abandon ME. Honor ME. Trust ME. Stick to MY truth in sickness and in health, in wealth or in poverty. And most importantly, never forsake ME. It was time to reclaim love for myself. I didn't need a man or a wedding ring. I needed to return to the love within myself. And to do that, I needed to promise to always give love to myself, regardless of who was in my life.

As the ukulele died down, I pulled out the piece of paper with my vows on it. I looked around the circle at humans who weeks before had been strangers and I felt so much love in my heart for them. Love for the shared memories we were making. Love for this beautiful beach town. Love for living out my Happy List and feeling at home in the world. There was love all around me for my taking, and it was about time I vowed to live life with a mission to soak up every single drop of it.

I stood back from the fire, and away from the heat of the flames and spoke the following vows to myself:

> I, Mel Miles, vow not to sabotage my own happiness. I give myself permission to enjoy life and not feel guilty for spending money or taking time for myself.

I, Mel Miles, vow to ALWAYS listen to the answers inside myself, rather than searching outside or looking for someone to make the decision for me.

I, Mel Miles, vow never to sacrifice my soul or freedom or physical well-being at the expense of serving others.

I, Mel Miles, vow never to edit my perspective/choices/feelings so that someone else will approve of me, including people I crave attention from.

I, Mel Miles, vow not to ignore or bottle up my feelings for the sake of appearing "strong." I will honor my feelings, be honest about them with others, and not push people away from my heart.

I, Mel Miles, vow to always choose telling the truth and turning toward my pain over being stuck in the trenches of shame and hiding my mistakes.

I, Mel Miles, vow to let love happen to me, not force it or try to change myself to make it work.

I, Mel Miles, give myself permission to enjoy emotional, spiritual, and physical connections in relationships without putting pressure on myself to make decisions about the future.

I, Mel Miles, vow to stay present to my pain. Instead of numbing, distracting, or otherwise turning away, I will turn toward it. I believe when we turn toward our pain, it sets us free.

I, Mel Miles, vow not to craft multiple versions of myself to fit into different circles, but rather to show up consistently wherever I go.

I, Mel Miles, vow to express my needs as they emerge and let others help fill them.

I, Mel Miles, vow to always speak my truth and use my authentic voice, even if it means causing conflict or losing relationships.

We ended the night swimming naked under only the light of the stars. In a foreign country. With strangers delightfully turned into new friends. Celebrating a love that wasn't birthed from romance—but birthed from within and shared in community.

CHAPTER 10: CHOOSE YOURSELF

I was softening into my Pause, or perhaps my Pause was softening me. Worry about being without a job wasn't keeping me up at night anymore. My mind was slowing down, and I consumed far less energy each day crafting stories to justify my Pause to skeptics (and myself)! In fact, what appeared to many outsiders as crazy... I was finding wildly fun. *Perhaps being a corporate escapee and societal misfit isn't so bad.*

From life with the Hacker Paradise community in Koh Lanta, Thailand, I continued to make my way to the places I had written on my Happy List after my phone call with DB. I spent a solo week in Paris, following the smell of chocolate croissants and reading self-helps books in the cobblestone cafes of the second arrondissement. Then I moved to Ireland, where I was lonely enough to sign up for a group tour of the Cliffs of Moher. Sometimes cheesy tour bus groups are exactly the medicine a soul needs to feel less alone in the world. I was thirty-two, single, divorced, and a motherless daughter. I imagined I was living like some people did after college, when they spend their savings from their college job on a wild adventure, for one last hurrah before they start adulting. Yet I was not a college student. I had had a respectable job. I recently owned a KitchenAid, a fully paid-for Honda Accord, and an expensive vacuum. But I had found myself wondering why I owned these things, and if they made me happy.

In a Dublin bar one evening I eavesdropped on a table of college students laughing hysterically. They seemed to not have a care in the world. *Why does the world approve of play so much when we're young?* I thought. We have societal permission to frolic around and "waste time." As youth, we are celebrated for living untethered and free, crafting imaginary worlds, dreaming big dreams, and making Happy Lists. Then somewhere along the way we became adults and got the message we had to "make the best use of time." We filled our days with outcome-oriented endeavors. Play became the icing on the cake: something you could indulge in when expectations were met, and lists ticked off. Deep in my bones it never felt quite right, but there didn't seem to be any other way.

I was amazed to learn that what felt like an act of grown-up rebellion was supported by convincing research. The psychiatrist Stuart Brown spent his career studying the relationship between play and mental and physical well-being. He transcribed more than 6,000 "play histories" of people from all countries and walks of life. In his bestselling book *Play: How It Shapes the Brain, Opens the Imagination, and Invigorates the Soul*, he unpacks the significant negative effect lack of play is having on society. Play, he writes, "is defined as purposeless, all-consuming, and fun."[14] His evidence shows adults who don't experience consistent play report more depression, chronic stress-related illness, and criminal behavior, in addition to fewer social skills and less intelligence, creativity, and ability to problem solve. He argues that a lack of play is a serious health risk to your body and mind, and "should be treated like malnutrition." If play is the cake you only eat on occasion, according to Dr. Brown, we all should be eating cake for breakfast every day!

After Dublin, I took a short flight to London, where my cousin Rebekah lived with her family. She would buy me day-of tickets to the theater, sit with me in a pub afterwards, and over fish and chips, listen to me ramble on about why Brock left me and why my Pause felt so damn scary.

"Follow these feelings to the end," she would say each time we met up for a girls' day. "Often in life we don't know what we don't know. Then something happens, and we have a chance to know it. And that knowing changes everything."

I didn't fully understand what she was talking about, but when my month in London ended, I traveled to the small island of Paros in Greece to put to words all the things I had spoken out loud to Rebekah. I sat on my balcony overlooking the sea and wrote a letter to the younger, more playful version of myself who didn't feel like she belonged at the Gates Foundation. I wrote a letter to Brock, saying all the things I wanted to but never had the courage to say when we were married. I wrote a letter to my mom. I even wrote my own obituary. Words were my medicine of choice to reconnect with the voice inside myself I seemed to have lost.

Each time I pulled my head up out of these words, I felt like a human with more access to my true wants, needs, and desires. And this access made it emotionally simpler to keep following the path of ease and moving my way down my Happy List. From Greece, I learned to sail in the British Virgin Islands. I attended an eight-day silent retreat. I ate cheese for dinner with no guilt. I meandered the castles of Europe, getting lost and not worrying if I would be late to anything. I took a course in sensuality and female sexual pleasure. I stayed up late dancing. My new persona was "Yes Mel." Yes Mel was willing to say yes to what she needed, wanted, or desired without shame or self-criticism.

HELL YES to not setting an alarm.

HELL YES to not obsessing over my calendar.

HELL YES to not making many plans or appointments.

HELL YES to not calling people back if I didn't want to.

HELL YES to wandering city streets with no agenda.

HELL YES to sitting in cafes and writing all the thoughts that passed through my brain.

HELL YES to afternoon naps with no shame.

HELL YES to new people.

HELL YES to spontaneous opportunities.

HELL YES to unfamiliar streets.

HELL YES to dancing in the kitchen for at least ten minutes a day.

HELL YES to taking the long way home and not being in a hurry.

HELL YES to my own joy.

I had no work identity, no home, and only the belongings in my suitcase, but I had started to feel like I was actually living. The problem was that with my location changing frequently, I had little consistency. Each day felt like a new decision about what to do with my time. I was uprooted and free, but still flustered. That's when sweet Susan, who I was still seeing virtually, said to me, "Mel, I think you would benefit from something to stay consistent each day. How about you create a morning routine? You know, something that can stay the same when everything else is changing."

"Um, no way in hell am I joining the 5:00 a.m. morning routine crew. This sounds like work," I said, skeptical.

"No, this isn't about getting up early or doing more. Try spending the first thirty minutes after you wake up not touching your phone. Instead, do something fun and that makes you feel happy. Imagine you were a millionaire with no worries. What would you wake up and want to do first?" she asked me.

I looked at her with a blank stare.

"You could journal, read a book, dance to a playlist, meditate, take a walk ... whatever. It's not supposed to feel like work. The goal is to do something that connects you to yourself and feels good before you engage with others each day. Think of it as filling your energy tank *before* you get up and start giving energy away."

Resistant of any formula, I came up with a compromise with Susan. I committed to spend the first hour of my day in a morning routine. However, the only two things I did consistently were answer these two questions in my journal:

1. How do I feel emotionally today?
2. How do I feel physically today?

I started out with a chart of "feelings words" Susan gave me and scribbled a few each morning in what became my "feelings journal." (This practice is now part of the Soulcation Workbook, which you can buy online at www.takeasoulcation.com/planner). Besides that, when meditation felt hard, I danced. When dance didn't feel quite right, I read. Sometimes I stared into my coffee and did nothing at all. The one thing that was consistent was for the first thirty minutes of my day, I wasn't touching my phone. I was connecting with self and doing something that I had an inkling would feel good—because feeling good was becoming my priority.

This morning routine was mundane, simple, and ordinary. But I started to feel conscious, connected, and in a deep, loving relationship with myself for the very first time. My heart was beginning to trust ease, and to choose to do more of what felt good. I didn't exactly know what was happening. Answering these two questions—day in and day out—and planning my day to respond compassionately to how I was feeling, was making everything in my life better. The societal conditioning I'd lived with my entire life still tried to tell me I had to tackle a list. But my emotional and physical sensations were telling me all I *really* had to do to have a good day was *listen* and *honor* them.

DO I HAVE TO GO BACK?

It was soon spring, six months since I'd set out with just a suitcase and a smartphone. My next stop was Israel, a place I'd heard about in thousands of church sermons and years of Christian school growing up. I hadn't been to church in a while, though. After Brock left and my Christian concept of "marriage is forever" shattered, I had no desire to. I figured if God was real, I would be able to find him floating on a plastic unicorn in Thailand or at a Parisian café as I talked to strangers. I was over Sunday services at a rented YMCA.

But here I was in Israel—the geographic home of God's people. When I checked into my Airbnb, the host pointed to a steel door and room with no windows. "It's called the bunker room. It's where you to go if the missile sirens go off," she said. "But don't worry, honey, this room will hold up against the worst."

She winked, dropped the key in my hand, and went on her way. I stepped outside on my balcony. My eyes were drawn to the words "fuck war" spray-painted in big, black letters on the building across the way. Beyond that was the blue water of the Mediterranean Sea. After unpacking, I opened my laptop and Googled "non-religious things you can you do in Tel Aviv." The first thing that came up were the city's world-renowned nightclubs.

Boom, that's it.

I slipped on a little black dress and walked past the Fuck War building, through the night market where street vendors were selling shakshuka, hummus, and freshly made falafels, and arrived at the nightclub. I felt a buzz in my body immediately—electric sparks pulsed in my fingers and toes. If the sparks had words, they would say, "Yes, Mel, this is fully living." I danced my heart out that first night. Sweat dripped down my legs. My hips rocked to the beat of Beyoncé. I felt the soft, sticky touch of human flesh. I heard lovers whisper tender words. I let a hot Israeli, dark-haired and dressed in all black, pull me into his arms and kiss me. I felt the pulse of my heart: soft, eager, and alive. I didn't even know this guy's name, but at the end of the night he squeezed me and said, "Keep your heart open, it's beautiful that way."

At 2:00 a.m. I stumbled onto the street drunk—not on alcohol, but on pure life bliss. Clearly all these years there was this pumping, playful, buzzing side of me. As I began to walk to my hotel, my phone vibrated.

"Dad, is everything okay?"

"Mel, you said you'd call when you landed. I never heard from you."

Shit. I forgot.

"I'm here, Dad, I made it. I'm having so much fun ..." I yelled over the music streaming out from the club.

"Oh good, good. I worry about you, Mel. You know that, right?" he said in his usual voice. "Have you decided when you're coming home yet?"

I'd been avoiding this question. I had told my family my Pause would be a few months. I knew my dad thought this was just a blip and I'd be returning, albeit slightly changed, to some semblance of my previous life. He wanted me to buy a house, land a slightly different flavor of job, find myself another partner, and put this whole season behind me.

"I'm really enjoying life, Dad. I'm happy here. I think I'll keep traveling a bit longer," I shouted into the phone.

"Um, so you don't have a ticket home yet?"

I could still feel the electrical currents of ease in my body. My heart was full and soft. The words "I'm happy here" had never been so true. I was changing on a cellular level. I was meeting a new version of me. And I liked her!

"I'm not going back to my old life, Dad," I said in a moment of courage. "Even when my Pause ends, things are going to be different."

Things are going to be different. I am going to be different. I couldn't ignore this truth.

My Soulcation was changing everything.

Things are going to be different. It was the first time I had uttered those words out loud. But I'd never sensed it so powerfully in my gut. My Pause was teaching me there was another way to live. I was intrigued. More than that, I wanted to hold onto this feeling as long as possible.

"Okay, Mel. Call me tomorrow. Let's talk about this more."

I hung up the phone and walked by the Fuck War building again. I couldn't help but wonder if not giving a fuck about war was actually a useful coping skill for living in Tel Aviv. Maybe I was going to have to not give a fuck what my dad thought in this what-next decision.

LIFE IS MEANT TO BE ENJOYED

Deep in your body and bones I suspect you hold the hope that life is meant to feel good. There are no suffering Olympics, friends.

No one gets a gold medal for tolerating more pain than the next human. Struggle is not something to brag about. After all, if your day-to-day life is noble but makes you feel miserable, is that how you want to live your life?

In the book *The Top Five Regrets of the Dying*, palliative care worker Bronnie Ware reminds us that one of the biggest regrets of dying people is that they didn't choose to enjoy life. Based on her research and experience interviewing hundreds of dying people, here are the top five regrets:

1. I wish I'd had the courage to live a life true to myself, not the life others expected of me.
2. I wish I hadn't worked so hard.
3. I wish I'd had the courage to express my feelings.
4. I wish I had stayed in touch with my friends.
5. I wish I let myself be happier.[15]

If you're anything like I was when I first read these, your soul is nodding and screaming, "Yes, I so wish I would let myself be happier!" This begs the question, *why do we fail to learn from the dying and continue to let ourselves have these regrets?*

I believe it's because we carry around some mash-up of small and big trauma—inherited from the world in which we grew up—that conditioned us to choose something or someone else *before ourselves*. As children, most of us unconsciously deployed whatever strategy worked to get love and attention from our primary caregiver. If, like me, you didn't have fully emotionally available parents, your coping mechanism likely involved leaving your own world—with your present needs, desires, and wants—to enter *their* world of needs, desires, and wants. And you likely carried this coping mechanism for finding love and safety into adulthood.

You have learned to choose meeting your kids' or spouse's needs ahead of your own. You have learned to choose meeting your boss's needs ahead of your own. You have learned to choose dealing with your inbox and mailbox, the mess on the kitchen table, and requests scribbled on sticky notes (or mental notes) before your own needs. Without doing the inner work of Soulcation, these coping mechanisms drive the ship.

These coping mechanisms didn't start with you, but the good news is you can let them end with you. Soulcation is about doing the work required to choose yourself in all the ways you never felt safe to (or never learned how to) from your family and society. You may be wondering, "Mel, what do you mean choose myself? That all sounds fine and good, but I already do that. That's not my problem. My problem is way bigger: It's stress and emotional overwhelm and panic—not lack of choosing myself."

Maybe that's true. But maybe it's not. I'd love you to approach this chapter with a gentle curiosity to consider—just consider—if there are areas of your life where it's not true. Are there parts of your life where you are not choosing a desire or inkling or perhaps a big, scary dream? I say this not to judge, but as my job. You've trusted me with your time on these pages, and I'm committed to leading you to more joy, play, and pleasure in life. In my experience, the work of choosing yourself has great power to heal anxiety, emotional overwhelm, and stress. And it's work that is never finished. You can always go deeper and deeper into yourself and discover new desires, longings, and delights. This is the hardest work I've ever done. There is no script or formula, but when you don't yet know how to choose yourself, here is what helped me.

CHOOSE YOURSELF BY LISTENING TO YOUR BODY

It's true what they say: The body keeps score. But more than that, the body usually knows before your mind does. Sensation is the language of the body. It grants us reams of information about ourselves—and how to choose ourselves—if we commit to learning its language.

After my dad called that night in Tel Aviv, I got terribly sick. I had diarrhea almost every day. I would wake up sweating in the middle of the night. I had to beg tour guides to stop at the next bathroom as I toured Jerusalem, the Dead Sea, and Jordan. I blamed it on bad street kebabs and constantly took Pepto Bismol, but deep-down I wondered if my body was reacting to not knowing what was next in life. When the gut pain and diarrhea didn't clear up, my friend Sarah said to me over Zoom during our weekly calls, "Mel, you know all this gut stuff might be emotional? You're going through some big changes; all this sickness could be your body's way of telling you it needs something."

Awareness of our body's sensations—or listening to our bodies—is a portal to choosing ourselves. Most of us struggle to choose ourselves because we are accustomed to living primarily in our minds. Our minds have patterns that run unconsciously and prime us to give more attention to the world around us than to our inner world. We have learned to override the sensations in our body and "keep on going." However, we are literally moving about the world not using fifty percent of our internal GPS system.

The human body doesn't really know the difference between physical and emotional pain. I'm simplifying the complex field of neuroscience here, but the pain of breaking an ankle is registered and processed not too differently from the pain of a heartbreak. To the nervous system, pain is pain. Listening to the sensations of your body can help you come into awareness and heal. Your body knows you're burned out before your mind does. Your body knows you are carrying around unprocessed grief before your mind does. Your body knows you are in a toxic relationship before your mind does. Your body will send a red flag before your mind will. Get quiet enough to listen to the language of bodily sensations and you will unlock one of the most important information sources to choose yourself.

Soul Hack: Give Your Sensations Words

I recommend exactly what my own somatic practitioner recommended to me, and what I still do to this day: Write down how you are physically feeling, using sensation words, every single day. To help you do this, use these questions:

- When does my body feel at its best?
- Where is my pain located?
- When do I notice my shoulders drop and my chest feel open?
- What does pleasure feel like in my body? When do I feel a nice tingling through my nervous system?
- What time of day do I feel the most energized?
- When does my body want a hug?
- And most importantly, if I could give words to my sensations, what would they say to me?

CHOOSE YOURSELF BY MOVING YOUR BODY

When we have A+ skills in overriding bodily sensations—and have lived this way most of our adult life—learning the language of our sensations is no easy feat. When I first started working with a somatic practitioner I had absolutely no experience trusting the voice of my body. I stared at her with glazed over eyes and inside my head thought, *this is all mumbo-jumbo, woo-woo shit that will never work.* I had run marathons, could get thirty minutes in at the gym like a pro, and had mighty fine posture in downward dog, after all. It wasn't like I was unfamiliar with moving my body. But here was the difference: I had never moved my body as a means for accessing its internal language of sensation. I had never moved my body in order to listen to it, or to find out what it needed. And I surely had never made life decisions based on what I heard back.

When I was in the early days of trying to "find the right station" to listen to my body's sensations, movement—and dance in particular—was my most helpful tool. I remember on my Pause attending a rooftop "movement workshop," led by an Argentinian artist named Josie. She opened by saying, "The most important part of this practice is non-judgment. There is no talking. The goal is to move your body however it wants to move with the music. Go to whatever shape feels good. Let whatever emotions are inside be expressed in movement." She turned the lights off and began playing songs arranged to the four natural elements: earth, wind, fire, and air.

This is so weird. I'm on a dark rooftop. With people I just met. And she wants me to move my body to the flow of my emotions. For all to see?

I started slowly, swaying my body with my hand on my chest as if I was a little girl in need of coddling. But soon I saw others across the room making big shapes and rapid movements—letting hands flail and their bodies shake with what I could only imagine was either deep anger or grief. One person sobbed. Another shook their hips in some sort of endless fiery frustration. As the moon rose and the dance continued, lit only by stars of the sky, I started to feel my body soften. I felt drawn to strong movements. I started taking up more space. My body was becoming an expression of my inner world, and I felt peace for the first time in years.

Soul Hack: Institute Dance Parties

In the journey to choose yourself, when in doubt, let yourself dance a) to express your emotions and b) to tap into the intuition of your bodily sensations. It's important you don't do this as a workout or a way to burn calories. Dance as a form of self-expression and self-curiosity. That said, it doesn't have to be a lengthy process or take tons of time. In between my client coaching sessions, I set a timer for ten minutes and dance to a few songs. Sometimes I move my body in dance as part of my morning routine. Now whenever I feel an uncomfortable emotion rushing through my body, I ask myself what movement it wants to make, then I dance it out. The practice feels weird at first, but here are a few questions to help get you started.

- What songs reflect the emotions you are feeling right now?
- How does your body want to move? Is it a soft/gentle movement or an aggressive movement?
- If your body was an element in this moment, what would it want to express: earth, wind, air, or fire?

- When during the day do you feel like your body most wants to move?

Lots of us exercise, but deep down what our body really wants is for us to move emotions through it.

CHOOSE YOURSELF BY ACCESSING YOUR SEXUAL PLEASURE

Pleasure is our birthright. It doesn't need to be earned or delayed for "someday." No matter what race, religion, or socioeconomic status you are, I believe you are inherently worthy of pleasure. Pleasure sets us apart from other mammals and it is ... well, *pleasurable*. One of the fundamental tenants of Soulcation is that there is an abundance of pleasure for our taking, and the problem is we stay on shore, observing rather than jumping in to swim in it.

In fact, far too many women suffer from what I call *Pleasure Anemia*. The lack of pleasure as well as the differential between male and female pleasure—both orgasmic and non-orgasmic—are appalling. Further, the female belief that we are not worthy of pleasure is a pandemic of ginormous magnitude. According to a 2016 study from the Archives of Sexual Behavior that looked at over 52,500 adults in the U.S., ninety-five percent of heterosexual men reported they usually or always orgasmed during sex, compared to sixty-five percent of heterosexual women.[16] Men are unequivocally experiencing more pleasure daily. There is a significant sexual pleasure gap, yes, but I believe this pleasure gap goes far beyond the bedroom. Women are afraid to choose themselves, and it has kept us blocked from our pleasure (and subsequently the creative energy we need to change the world and design a life we don't need a vacation from).

My story is unique. I was raised in the Christian "purity movement," married my very first boyfriend and first kiss, and was a virgin until my wedding day. After my divorce at thirty-one years old, I felt lost on how to approach intimacy again. I used to believe the pinnacle of sex was the male orgasm. In my marriage, sex was fine but rarely mind-blowingly amazing. It was quick and animalistic—and on occasion I would even fake an orgasm to get us moving onto the next thing. I had accepted I was no sex goddess. I was fine with plain vanilla sex. If he was happy, I was happy. But you can't reap the full benefits of Soulcation without activating your body's innate ability to experience, savor, and enjoy the pleasure that is your birthright. This was scary territory for me. And I knew I couldn't do it alone. I signed up for a coaching program I found while scrolling Instagram (how the pros do it, clearly) with Jasmine Rose of Humble Wild Wellness, all about reconnecting to our womb: the pleasure center of our female bodies. We called my journey "mission pleasure liberation" and she met with me week after week as we explored the junk drawer of my womb and began to unearth all the ways I had learned to deny myself pleasure.

I remember the first time I had a "pleasure ceremony." I bought a cervical wand, fancy body oil, and a $350 silk bra from Neiman-Marcus. *Crazytown, I know.* I arranged my room with cozy pillows and lavender scented candles and began gentle massaging my breasts, then moved down to my yoni, then dipped my fingers inside to feel the ribbed tissue that had been without touch for over a year at that point. I went ever so slowly, noticing the sensations and vibrations with every stroke of my fingers. I used to only reach to self-pleasure practices in moments of stress where I rushed to "get off." But this time I was approaching it with intentionality, consistency, and a radical new self-responsibility to keep the fire of pleasure lit within me. Yes, I hoped to share pleasure with another person again soon, but in order to not fall into the "new partner, same patterns" trap, I first had to do the work of reclaiming my relationship with pleasure. Pleasure needed to start with ME. And I needed to believe choosing pleasure was choosing myself.

I want to pause here to say there are so many ways to tap into the essence of sexual pleasure outside the bedroom. In fact, for many women the bedroom is the least likely place to feel comfortable enough to choose ourselves and thereby make our needs paramount. The first time I attempted sex after my marriage ended, I froze. It was in a treehouse on the most romantic private island in Thailand where there was a large soaking tub, a private pool, and a luxurious bed. Yet the vulnerability of the moment and my doubts around pleasure being my birthright sent me into fear, and I felt paralyzed. I was getting in my own way and blocking myself from pleasure.

No matter where you are along this pleasure journey, a great way to practice choosing yourself is by developing a strategy to tap into your sexual energy outside the bedroom.

Soul Hack: Bring Sexual Energy into Your Daily Tasks

The goal here is to make everything in your life more pleasurable. By tapping into sexual energy *outside the bedroom*, you are awakening your own internal flame for activating pleasure. Everyone will exude this energy differently, but here are some questions to guide you on your own energetic exploration:

- How can I bring more pleasure into daily chores, like cooking or doing the dishes?
- How can I bring more pleasure into getting ready for and being at work, so work feels more juicy, delicious, and wonderful?
- What would it look like to bring sexual energy into my home, so I can access more pleasure outside the bedroom?
- How can I bring more pleasure into the last hour before I go to bed? What non-sexual routines will help invoke pleasure?

Let your body love what it loves. Pleasure is your birthright. And it's ripe for your taking.

CHOOSE YOURSELF BY SWITCHING THINGS UP

"If something isn't working, switch it up. You can decide now. And then decide differently later." These were the words gently delivered by sweet Susan when I was trying to decide when to end my Pause. It wasn't just the ending with which I was struggling. I didn't know what would come after my Pause. Each time I changed locations I had to figure out where to get groceries, where to do yoga, how to use the city's transportation system, and what app the country used for food delivery. Then there was the mental energy of meeting new people, even in intentional communities like Hacker Paradise. The months were stacking up, and the energetic baggage of moving around was accumulating. My body was telling me it was time to stop. I knew I didn't want to go back to my old life, but I still had no idea what an alternative new life could include.

I was still in Tel Aviv; it had been a month since my dad's first call. I walked down to the white sand of the Mediterranean Sea and found a quiet spot all by myself. To my right I could see the ancient cobblestone buildings of Jaffa, and to my left were a few miles of soft, gentle waves and sand. I had come to the water's edge to sit in stillness and to listen for ... well, something that would resemble an answer to the question I was dreading: What next? I sat there for hours. I listened to the waves. I watched the birds. I noticed the few tourists that walked past me to the very end of the beach. The sky started to get dark. The moon rose. My body still didn't move. Despite all the space I had created in my life, I felt uncertain, indecisive, and helpless. Continuing to travel felt like pushing my body past its limits. But going back to a similar life as before would feel like failure, as if the whole Pause was for nothing.

My body was getting cold. I looked out into the darkness and felt the danger of this place, and the danger of being alone. That's when sweet Susan's words came back to me. "You can't make a wrong decision, Mel. There is no right and wrong anymore. You don't have to commit to anything. You can try something, and when it doesn't work out, you can try to switch things up again."

I was a woman who could switch up my socks when they got holes in them or buy new throw pillows for the couch. But until my Pause, I never gave myself permission to switch up the real, important things in life. *Could I not be sure about something, and switch it up anyway?*

Soul Hack: Switch Something Up

You can have savings, then spend it down and not have savings. You can be in a relationship, then not be in a relationship. You can be employed by a company, and then go off and start your own business. You can move to a new city, and then when it's not working, you can switch it up and move. You can purchase a house, and then when the universe calls you to live your dream life in Europe, you can sell, make zero profit, and still be blissfully happy. You can do all of this because you have the power to choose yourself. And when you know you have this power, you can give yourself constant permission slips to switch things up.

You can have a goal and then change it. You can want something for a long time, and then want something else. You can pivot your entire life in one direction, and then when your body tells you it's not working, pick everything up and head in the opposite direction. When you know you can always switch things up, you will never be paralyzed by a decision, because you know there is always another decision you can make to honor your highest good.

When we aren't familiar with the feeling of choosing ourselves (or haven't been taught how to), we might not realize there is something in our life we want to switch up. If you are struggling to choose yourself and faced with indecision, here are some prompts for self-exploration:

- What no longer feels like it's working in your life?
- What decision in the past do you secretly wish you could undo?
- If you could change your mind about one thing, what would it be?

- If you follow your fear to the end, what is it trying to say to you? And if you really believed you could change your mind, what would you do?

CHOOSE LOVE

The one thing I haven't told you this whole chapter is that the act of choosing yourself is really about choosing love. When we choose to love ourselves radically and unconditionally, we evoke love in all dimensions of our life. The core of all emotional exhaustion—whether it be overwhelm, anxiety, or burnout—is the basic fear that you are not loveable. Taking conscious action to choose yourself is the way you meet this fear with love.

This act is not a skill one must learn. Rather, it is a remembrance. Soulcation, dear sister, is the art of remembering something you have always known. You know how to love. It's the medicine, when directed at yourself, that will set you free.

Play, pleasure, and rest are your birthrights. Never stop choosing yourself. Your life literally depends on it.

PART III:

HOW TO DESIGN A LIFE YOU DON'T NEED A VACATION FROM

CHAPTER 11: THE 7-STEP SOULCATION FRAMEWORK (AKA FUN-WORK)

I have a love-hate relationship with frameworks. Frameworks are, by definition, a conceptual model intended to support expansion or creation of something new. But after devouring frameworks in self-help books, podcasts, and nearly all the Google articles on "anxiety attacks" written between 2016 and 2018—the result being no improvement with my panic attacks—I was skeptical of any framework out there. I had tried them. They had failed me. Yet on my Pause I had thrown out the script for what I *should* be doing and hadn't had one single panic attack. Was it possible I could ignore the advice I learned growing up and in doing so, finally live the life I always wanted? Was turning inwards and trusting myself medicine for an anxious soul?

These were the questions that swirled through my head as the weeks went on in Israel, still in that same apartment looking out on the Fuck War building, contemplating what to do next. The dissonance of my anxiety subsiding through such an unconventional means ... that wasn't lost on me. It was undeniable, even to my scientific mind, that tossing out my old frameworks was getting me somewhere. After years of living with anxiety, I started posting on social media about my healing. I got responses like:

- Did your panic attacks really stop?
- Do you really feel like you've accepted all your losses?

- It hasn't been that long ... you mean you're not stuck in the grief of death and divorce anymore?
- How did you get unstuck? Can you tell me what worked for you?
- Do you think your change is permanent, or will the stress just come back when you're working again?

Even friends back in Seattle were skeptical. Underneath their questions I could sense an unspoken doubt that a playful, free way of living was sustainable. It seemed their underlying belief was you couldn't be an adult and live a life that feels *playful* and *fun* every day. It was never said directly to me, but I felt it in the air. Like the time an old college friend texted me, "Mel, when are you going to stop having fun and return home?" Or when an acquaintance wrote me a private Instagram message that said, "I see you're having the time of your life, Mel, but remember you're not living real life. Get prepared for the stress and anxiety to return."

My body tensed at the words stress, anxiety, and return. It felt like a cruel prophecy. Yet part of me wondered if acquaintance was right. Perhaps her words scared me because they made sense. Did I spend all my savings on this Pause only to return to the same jam-packed calendar and anxiety-filled version of myself? Would my Soulcation only serve as a temporary escape? And even worse, would the panic attacks start up again? While these slighting messages threw me for a loop, it was also the first time I considered the difference between a temporary escape from our pain and the journey we all must take to *heal our pain*. From my balcony in Israel, I had no simple answer for the internal shifts that were leading to the external healing in my life. But I wondered if I was onto something that could be replicated.

SOULCATION FUN-WORK

The diarrhea-filled days in Tel Aviv ended two years ago now. In the interim I've combed all sorts of literature, going deep into neuroimmunology, psychology, and spirituality. I've read things from Western and Eastern perspectives—and consumed teaching from people with whom I agree and disagree. I've watched some self-help gurus in my space quickly shoot to stardom, only to have to swallow the hard pill in their own lives that positive thinking will only take you so far. I've conducted interviews with women in over twelve countries on how they design their lives. And I've taken all I've learned and launched a full suite of services at https://takeasoulcation.com where I guide women from their own burnouts to lives they don't need a vacation from. I've experimented with all sorts of things—from ayahuasca with a shaman in the Mexican jungle to meditation with nuns in the hills above Silicon Valley. I've listened to pastors, PhDs, parents, and peasants with the same curiosity, committed to trying their ideas in my own life and seeing how my body reacts.

What follows is the closest I've come to my version of a framework. It's what I call a FUN-work: my way to formalize the art of throwing out the things no longer serving you so you can really make your life fun. Unlike other frameworks, I based it on only good, juicy, soul-filled things that don't make you clench your jaw with that, "Gah, not another thing to do" feeling. I wanted to create a way to help sink into rest, play, and pleasure as the gateway to "doing the inner work" of transformation so many therapists talk about. When we push ourselves, our ego and inner critic start to take over, and change is never possible when the inner critic is in charge. It's only when we go softly and gently that we can change behaviors, and our lives, from the inside out.

It's time you let your life be full of play and fun, sister. And here is my best attempt at showing you how to do that.

SOULCATION FUN-WORK

1. Start with joy (create a Happy List)
2. Observe emotions (get curious)
3. Unplug (make space for YOU)
4. Listen to your body (give yourself what you need)
5. Follow your intuition (trust, play, and rest as tools for healing)
6. Unlearn limiting beliefs (rewrite old memos)
7. Live a life you don't need a vacation from (stop waiting and take the leap)

S - START WITH JOY: CREATE A HAPPY LIST

I know what it's like when nothing feels good. I get it. When you're at rock bottom, descending into your dark night of the soul, you can't even muster the energy to think of what would feel joyful. To Start with Joy feels unreachable. Yet when we start doing the inner FUN-work with self-kindness rather than self-criticism, we flip our entire approach to healing. Joy is no longer an end goal; it is medicine. We begin to pay attention to the sensations of joy in the body (even if it's just for short moments) in humor, amusement, delight, comfort, festivities, luxury, treats, and refreshment. We put attention into planning ways we can connect—and embody—these sensations on a daily basis. We let these moments, even if they are just fleeting, help us soften, open, and trust that we can choose ourselves, and choose ease.

Start with Joy is not about always feeling joy: it's about mindset. We *Start with Joy* as a way of our body telling our mind we are worthy of rest, play, and pleasure. We *Start with Joy* so we can stop taking things so seriously. We *Start with Joy* so we can use each playful moment to support the life transformation we're being called more deeply into. We *Start with Joy* because our old lists aren't serving us anymore, and most women are in desperate need of a Happy List.

Joy doesn't come after the next milestone, achievement, or task. It comes when we believe we are worthy of it and start choosing it. When we take actions that reinforce a feeling of ease, we start to feel it more. Our identities change as our actions do. *Start with Joy*, and you'll find your belief about being a person worthy of constant joy shifts.

FUN-work Reflections:

- What one thing do I KNOW will bring me joy this week?
- What experiments do I want to design to explore more of what brings me joy?
- What permission slip(s) do I need to give myself to support an "experimentation mindset" with my relationship with JOY?

O - OBSERVE EMOTIONS: GET CURIOUS

We've talked about emotions and feelings a lot in this book, because I believe they are the gateway to the soul. Access your deepest feelings and you access your deepest wisdom. Observe your feelings and you are looking at what makes you YOU. Write down your feelings each day and you have a road map to what you need.

The art here is to learn how to step back and *Observe Emotions,* not judge them. Observing or witnessing emotions leads to insight. Seeing yourself *only as your feelings* leads to overwhelm. It's the difference between running *with a feeling* and letting a feeling *run you.* The FUN-work is to start noticing the difference—and honing the skill of being a gentle observer rather than a critical judge of your feelings.

The art of *Observing Emotions* is to name them. Write them down every morning and repeat this mantra: "I see you. You are welcome here." (It sounds strange, but talking to your feelings like they are a person is a great way to see them as simply a *part of you*—not all of you.)

Play the role of a mother to your feelings; gently witness them instead of wrangling them or stuffing them in a box. You do not need to make meaning yet or have answers. You just need to stop ignoring the very thing your body and soul is screaming at you *not* to ignore.

FUN-work Reflections:

- You usually experience more than one emotion at once. What are two opposing emotions/feelings that don't make sense to you, but which you feel most strongly right now?
- What is the emotion you want to feel more of this week?
- What usually evokes this emotion in you?
- What can you add or take away from your schedule to support accessing this emotion more?
- Here are some specific questions you can ask:

Anger	What boundaries are being crossed that I need to reclaim to fully experience joy and rest?
Fear	What fears do I have around rest that I need to
Joy	What are the gifts I'm giving myself that I can celebrate?
Sadness	What grief is coming up about how I've denied myself something I've needed in the past?
Sexual/ creative energy	Where or how can I access more pleasure?

U - UNPLUG: CREATE SPACE FOR YOU

Does scrolling your phone right when you wake up or before bed feel good? Does rushing around all day with the next item on your list on your mind make you feel the way you want to? Do you want to live life constantly thinking, "I don't have enough time today" or "I don't have any blank space in my calendar all week"?

I'm right there with you in enjoying the technology we have access to. But constant connection depletes the soul. It's not healthy for humans to always *be on*. We live in a time when people have far less white space in their lives than any other time in human history, and all the evidence points to that lack making us physically and mentally sick.

One of the most important steps in this FUN-work is to create white space for YOU. I call it "work" for a reason: It requires unplugging in some radical ways. *Unplugging* means saying a lot more "hell no" when you would usually put a smile on your face and say yes.

Unplugging means intentionally carving out time to do NOTHING.

Unplugging means not checking your phone for the first thirty minutes of the day.

Unplugging means blocking ME time on the calendar and making sure everyone knows you can't be reached.

And yes, *Unplugging* involves taking yourself on a solo date, or going away for a weekend or even a full week by yourself.

Ultimately, *Unplugging* requires you to pull back from whatever it is you are addictively connected to (tech, work, taking care of other people, pick your vice...), because it's stopping you from hearing your soul's voice.

If you don't unplug, you won't change. It's as simple and difficult as that.

FUN-work Reflections:

The best ideas often arrive in the white space where we can think, wander, and let our brains make connections across different experiences and conversations. Here are some questions to help you plan your *Unplugging*:

- How can I build white space into my calendar this week?
- When during the week is it possible to set aside some "no technology" time?

- When am I going to get away for a night (or weekend) to have dedicated time to myself?
- When will I turn off my phone or email this week?

Action Steps to Kickstart your Soulcation:

- Put at least one or two white space appointments in your calendar each week (just as you would schedule other appointments).
- Put a block on your calendar for when you will take "digital off time" and not be on your phone/email.
- Tell your family and people you live with about these new white space commitments and ask them to support you in keeping them.

L - LISTEN TO YOUR BODY: GIVE YOURSELF WHAT YOU NEED

The FUN-work principle my clients come back to time and time again when they get stuck is this: *Give yourself what you need.* When you "don't know what to do," or you aren't sure what you need, *Listen To Your Body*. The physical cues and sensations in your body, such as tension in your shoulders after a long day at your computer, a tightening of the jaw when you're anxious, or an elevated heart rate (like I had at my doctor's before my panic attack) are the nervous system's way of signaling for attention and care. When we muscle through these cues in the name of productivity or loyalty, we're not only denying ourselves the care that will make us physically and emotionally well, but we're ignoring the cues intended to help us live a life we don't need a vacation from.

Ignoring physical cues is one of the root causes of burnout and emotional exhaustion. Unmet needs get stored in our bodies, sometimes for weeks or years if not tended to. As a result, what started as a small need can evolve into chronic back pain, headaches, insomnia, gut issues, or a host of other chronic disease. I have come to believe there is a powerful link between our emotional world and physical well-being. Unmet emotional needs stay stuck in our bodies and ultimately, manifest as physical symptoms. I've seen dozens of clients improve their physical well-being by doing the powerful work of committing to this step of giving themselves the rest, sleep, food, kindness, slowness, connection, or play they need. The essence of Soulcation is an invitation to tend to our body's physical cues and trust we are safe to pause our plans and give ourselves exactly what we need. When we stop ignoring the cues the voice of our body sends to us, we find a newfound freedom.

FUN-work Reflections:

- What sensations do I currently feel in my body as I plan out my week?
- What is my body telling me it needs this week?
- What is one way I can silence my "mind voice" and let my "body voice" lead this week?
- What restful, playful activities will support the flow of energy and emotion through my body?

F - FOLLOW YOUR INTUITION: TRUST PLAY AND REST AS TOOLS FOR HEALING

Perhaps it's been a long time since you listened to your intuition. Remember, intuition is the ability to understand something immediately, without relying on conscious reasoning. It's that "body knowing" that propels you to act even when it doesn't logically make sense.

If you're like most humans, you have a whole boardroom of voices in your head that want a say in making decisions: the inner critic, the disciplined coach, the judgmental parent pressuring you to do something regardless of fear, and the voice of that toxic ex or demanding boss telling you you're not enough. Likely unknowingly, you let these voices guide how you navigate life. They help you come up with a plan for what you should be doing. You execute. You feel exhausted executing. So, you go up to your mind to check in with another voice, asking it what you should be doing differently. For many people, this mental loop of checking in with the boardroom of voices continues, and guides their entire life. However, the problem here is your intuition—the very thing that holds everything you need to guide your life—is left out.

The work of Soulcation is to filter out the voices that don't have your best life in mind, and hone the voice of your intuition. In the world today, it is easier to say a polite YES than it is to scream FUCK NO to unrealistic norms and standards. The fear of not belonging—or heaven forbid, of becoming a societal misfit—keeps us tolerating voices in our head we don't even like that much. Sometimes these voices are so loud, all-consuming, and powerful we can't even hear our own intuition. This, sisters, is the problem worth solving before any other. And it's why slowing down, taking a Soulcation, and carving out an obnoxious amount of white space in life is so important to rising to new levels in your life. Play and rest are your gateways to reconnect with your intuition, because they both require being present with the body. And when we are present in our body, we begin to hear the voice of our intuition say things that make no sense to our rational mind but feel exactly right. Our body lets out a big sigh and says, "Yes, yes, that crazy thing; that's exactly it."

When we fail to make time for play and rest, we're missing out on one of the greatest sources of knowledge and power we have. It's no different than starving ourselves of sleep or food. Ignoring our intuition is like slowly starving ourselves to death. And turning toward our intuition and giving ourselves whatever it is telling us it wants is the work of Soulcation. This FUN-work step is all about letting your intuition guide you to play, rest, and yes, even a full day in bed when the mind might call it "lazy," and not feel shame about it. After all, sister, your life literally depends on this.

FUN-work Reflections:

- What is my intuition trying to tell me?
- How can I create space for stillness and silence and listen to my inner voice this week?
- What would I be doing differently if I trusted my intuition?
- What is my intuition telling me to say no to or not do this week?

U - UNLEARN LIMITING BELIEFS: REWRITE OLD MEMOS

Limiting beliefs are sneaky. I think of them as tax documents you file deep down in that ugly hall closet filing cabinet. You don't ever take them out to reread them, yet they've been in the filing cabinet for so long, you don't even stop to consider what you could do with that closet if they were gone. It's an accepted belief that you *have to* keep them around.

Limiting beliefs have power. They nestle themselves deep into our subconscious and make sure we follow their edicts. We pick them up at an early age, like osmosis, from family, society, religion, and the patriarchy. Examples of beliefs I've heard frequently from my clients that often need to be rewritten include:

- I can only rest once I've accomplished everything on my list.
- I have to earn my right to rest and play.
- Life is supposed to be hard, not full of pleasure.
- I am being "selfish" (or will be called selfish by others) if I put my needs and desires first.
- If I choose to slow down and rest, my family and/or career will unravel.
- Fun and play can come if I have time "left over."
- I can't quit my job without knowing what's next.
- I must always be moving forward in life.
- I've already committed to someone/something; I can't change my mind now.

As we grow into adulthood, these beliefs can become so second nature we don't ask one of the most life-changing questions: "What if this belief really isn't true?"

When was the last time you paused to ask yourself if the thing you believed you needed to be happy really was true? Not asking this question is at the root of a lot of stress and pain. The field of neuroscience shows subconscious beliefs (i.e. beliefs we live by but aren't often forefront in our minds), influence up to eighty to ninety percent of our actions.[17] This means if we're feeling trapped or stuck in life, we need to go deeper than usual, under the conscious surface of our lives, to question the beliefs that feel as true to us as paying our taxes.

Subconscious beliefs share four common key elements:

- First, the way you learned to feel safe in the world
- Second, the way you make meaning out of life events
- Third, the story and meaning you attach to core negative emotions
- And fourth, the mental "plan" you have crafted for your life

Because subconscious beliefs exist in the deepest, most underground layers of our lives, if you want to design a life you don't need a vacation from, you're going to need to deeply examine your unconscious beliefs about rest, play, and pleasure (along with your life overall). Examining one's beliefs is a lifetime practice, and there is no formula, but the tool I teach my one-on-one clients that has most rapidly transformed their happiness is what I call "The Four Observations." The Four Observations is a sequential line of inquiry intended to help the mind access its unconscious programs and consider another way. It's best done by taking at least two minutes to write out the answers to each question before moving onto the next. I always tell my clients that since The Four Observations is a tool to get you out of your *activated mind* and into the *quiet unconscious mind,* it's important to not just think about your answers but write them out. This lets you step back and be an observer of them. Here are the lines of inquiry:

- Observation #1: How does holding this belief make you feel?
- Observation #2: How does holding this belief make you act?
- Observation #3: How do you want to feel?
- Observation #4: How do you want to act?

Next time you feel emotional overwhelm or are heading into an uncomfortable emotional tunnel, try the Four Observations.

Letting go of old subconscious beliefs isn't always the most fun part of the FUN-work, but it's mission critical to being able to access the embodied, present, lifesaving play we all need. In fact, the secret to happiness no one tells you is that you most likely don't need to change your actions to be happier: You need to change your subconscious beliefs. One of my favorite authors, Joe Dispenza, says it well: "In order to change your life, you need to change your mind."

FUN-work Reflections:

- Growing up, what was *your parents' opinion on* the role of fun and play in their lives?
- What ways do you currently participate in fun and play in your life?
- What do you wish was different about the amount or type of play and rest you have in your life?

- Select one belief you have about rest, play, or pleasure (you can use the list of example client beliefs in the section above) and write down responses to The Four Observations.
    - How does holding this belief make you feel?
    - How does holding this belief make you act?
    - How do you want to feel?
    - How do you want to act?

L - LIVE A LIFE YOU DON'T NEED A VACATION FROM

Let's be honest. You likely picked up this book because you love vacations. You get pleasure from not only being on them, but also planning them and reminiscing about them afterwards. Perhaps you sometimes think about the younger version of you on vacation. You would wake up in Paris, without a map or plans for the day, and have the time of your life wandering the streets and stopping in sidewalk cafes. There were no kids or timelines or people to check in on back home. You liked that version of you, and you secretly want to find her again.

The whole point of a Soulcation is to help you embody this playful, romantic, spontaneous, Parisian version of you, and welcome her into your everyday life. And in order to do this, you need to be able to do three things on the regular.

Build the muscle of self-celebration. Celebrate your wins, especially the small ones that the world doesn't validate you for. This will provide a sense of lightness and fun, and a deep sense of worthiness to your life. This could look like eating reserved-for-special-occasions food, throwing yourself a party, taking yourself on a date, or creating a "celebration wall" in your home.

Practice choosing yourself. Meet your needs, desires, and wants. It can look as simple as canceling a meeting because you got news that made you sad. Or it may look like asking your partner to stop and listen to your feelings, help you cook dinner, or give you a night off because you need time to move through something that's weighing on you emotionally.

Become familiar with and confident in the art of letting go. The FUN-work framework is designed to support you in letting go of old identities, beliefs, and ways of being that aren't the most authentic and most fun version of you.

You may not arrive at this final step without releasing some friends, a shit ton of habits, a handful of subconscious limiting beliefs, and for some, even a partner, job, or city. But I'm here to say, these courageous acts of letting go are the very things that will guide you to waking up one morning, seeing this book on the shelf, and saying to yourself, "Yes, I did it. I'm actually living a life I don't need a vacation from."

FUN-work Reflections:

- What can you celebrate and "brag" on yourself about this week?
- What rest and play felt good for your soul this week?
- What do you want to say no to and/or do less of this week?
- If you didn't care what anyone else thought of you, what would you do?
- What can you do this week that feels like a vacation?
- What would you do if you weren't afraid?

CHAPTER 12: LET IT SHIFT

I stared helplessly into the Zoom screen. My recently hired career coach, Lisa, was on the other side. I was still in the same apartment in Tel Aviv, but my diarrhea continued with a vengeance. I regularly woke up fatigued, even after eight hours of sleep. Sometimes I would walk the city's Mediterranean boardwalk and my heart would race, and palms would sweat. I would find myself in full-on anxiety right in the middle of paradise. My face was broken out beyond what the best makeup could cover. The sensations in my body reminded me of the days prior to my panic attack at the Gates Foundation. Now, though, my bank account was at an all-time low and I was going to have to face my father's question: ***Now what?***

"Mel, let's do an exercise," Lisa said. "I'm going to ask you two questions. I'll set a timer for sixty seconds and I want you to fill in the blanks. The only rule is you have to write down the first things to come to mind," she said with a smile. "All right, complete this sentence: *When I let people love me, they* ________________ ____."

I took a deep breath and scribbled down the following:

abandon me
hurt me
reject me
fail to be there for me when I need them most
use me
take advantage of me
ignore my feelings

I reread my words for a minute. Love and I were not on the best terms. "All right, next question," Lisa went on. *"When I love people I ____ ______________."*

> *go out of my way to anticipate and meet their needs*
> *give them all my time and energy*
> *make efforts to stay connected*
> *am loyal to them*
> *want them to be easy on themselves*
> *want them to have their needs met*
> *want them to be happy*

"Hmmmm ..." Lisa whispered, with a knowing look on her face. Clearly what I gave in love and what I expected to receive back were vastly different.

"Your beliefs about love are going to shape everything about your future life, Mel," Lisa went on to say. "From my perspective, the real problem is not what you tell your dad. It is if you can love yourself with the same love you've been giving to other people your whole life."

I tilted my head down and gazed at my hands. "I don't know if I can..." I whispered.

I had proven to myself I could Soulcation. I had traveled solo to twelve countries, lived in four international co-living communities, finished my memoir, learned to sail, lived off the land, and most importantly, checked most things off my original Happy List. I had taken a Grand Pause and felt a happiness inside me I hadn't felt in a long time. It felt damn good. But would my body feel safe enough to stay here—in the Soulcation way? Or was this season of fun and play about to become just a memory? Not knowing which way this would all go scared me shitless (and I had constant diarrhea to prove it).

"Mel," Lisa gazed into my eyes over Zoom. "I know you're contemplating lots of options: returning to the U.S., getting a job again, settling in a new home, launching your own business. Promise me for just this next week you pause all thinking about these next steps."

I stared back at her, confused. I was paying her good money to help me make these decisions.

"I have no doubt these decisions will get made. But you won't fully trust them if you don't trust—and love—yourself first. That's why your homework for this week is to sit with these two questions: *What if the love you're so good at giving to others, you gave to yourself?*

And what if you thought about 'what next' not as choosing a job or home, but choosing the deepest things you love?"

I wasn't sure I could do it this way. I was used to job descriptions and pro-con lists.

I signed off Zoom and stared out the window in frustration. When I'd chosen love in the past, bad things happened. Brock left me unexpectedly. My mom died. I had a panic attack. *Could I have a life I loved, and that was full of love, post-Pause?*

THE SECRET TO GETTING UNSTUCK: REPLACE YOUR ACHIEVEMENT GOALS WITH FEELINGS GOALS

As a recovering workaholic, I learned one of the most transformative things of my life during my Pause: to rewrite my outcome goals as feelings goals. Let me tell you up front: In the beginning it will feel super weird. If you've spent any time in the corporate world, like I had at the Gates Foundation, you're likely skilled at developing goals to demonstrate your value and track progress. Even if you don't work for a company, I suspect you also have a system for writing personal goals you want to achieve in a period of time. When I look back at my role at the Gates Foundation, a big part of my job was to define clear, measurable, and quantifiable goals for our investments in Africa. I was good at it. But I think I loved all my goal-setting work because it provided a way for me to escape my present reality and live in the future. I could use my mind to think about, plan for, and manage the future. It was necessary work, don't get me wrong, but I became addicted to future-thinking (and there is enough evidence now to show future-thinking is a root cause of anxiety).[18] I would obsess over goals: how I could push myself harder, how I could achieve them, and what the next goal would be after the current one was complete. It became a vicious cycle of always wanting something that wasn't in my present reality. I became familiar with living in my head—in a version of the future I projected in my mind—rather than in the present moment right in front of me.

Goals are important. But a dysfunctional relationship with goals can wreak havoc on our life. We achieve goals, get a dopamine hit, and then need more goals and more dopamine to keep feeling good about ourselves. Soon, we are addicted to this vicious cycle, and it becomes that elusive pot at the end of the rainbow we can never find. We need to work even harder to feel success. Our minds override our bodies. We push ourselves past our limit, all to feel that high and validation from when we achieve a goal. But here's the truth with this cycle: We are not just chasing a goal. We are chasing a FEELING.

In her book *The Desire Map,* author Danielle LaPorte writes, "We've been taught that the winning game is with logic and strategy and thinking our way to success ... But when you set a goal, you're not actually chasing that goal—you're chasing a feeling. The power is in the heart, and we have to relearn how to create from that place."[19]

The idea of designing your life around feelings goals—or the way you want to feel most of your waking (and working) hours—reverses this cycle. It requires you to start with the end in mind—the feeling you want to feel—and think through how you can embody the energy of that feeling in your present reality. To be honest, flipping the script like this was quite challenging for me. I studied Danielle's writing and work on what she called "core desired feelings" (or the core feeling we seek through an external action), and started journaling my way through the questions in her book:

- What are your core desires?
- When do you currently experience these core desired feelings in your life? Where do you most often feel distant from them?
- What brings you alive, enlivens you, reminds you of whom you are?
- What depresses your spirit, weighs you down, and sucks your energy?
- What time of day do you feel your core desired feelings? What are you usually doing then?

Here is what came up for me when I homed in on what I most wanted to feel:

I want to feel free.
I want to feel a sense of openness and expansiveness.
I want to feel like I can use my voice.
I want to feel calm, confident, and valued.
I want to feel love—and receive love.
I want to feel a sense of connection and wonder.
I want a life that feels good and happy and not like work.

When I reflected on everything I wrote, it came down to three core desired feelings: connection, adventure, and freedom. I looked at the list and smiled. For the first time I saw that I had a life purpose oriented around *feelings*, not achievements. I didn't have to rely on my achievements to give me a certain feeling. I could set a goal around how I wanted to feel and put my energy toward evoking that feeling in my everyday life.

I wasn't exactly sure how it was going to work, but the words *connection, adventure*, and *freedom* soon became my north stars. Instead of thinking through what job I wanted next, I reversed the process and started brainstorming the activities and lifestyle that would cultivate the feelings I wanted to feel. Things like my morning routine (connection), continually visiting new places (adventure), and setting my own schedule (freedom) came to mind. I soon had the beginnings of a new sort of map for my post-Pause life.

Yes, we all benefit from having goals. They give us direction. But we get to decide whether that direction is focused on the future (and what we want to achieve), or on the present (and how we want to feel). Ideally we are all striving for some combination of the two. Feeling and achievement goals are like the yin and the yang. Coffee and cream. Moon and sun. Wine and cheese. You need both to make life full and yummy. If you find yourself way too deep in the achievement-focused camp (like I did for so many years), setting feelings goals is a great strategy. And my guess would be if you have a dry mouth, it's because you haven't added the milky, buttery, silky cream of feelings goals to your life's coffee yet. But it's never too late to start.

THE ONLY WAY IS THROUGH

Over the course of the next month, my feelings goals, along with continued work with Lisa, helped me chart a new direction. I would not return to Seattle. Instead, I would prioritize remote work to honor my desire to be free and adventurous, and I would prioritize finishing this book—because writing connected me to myself and fueled meaningful connections. However, if the book was going to become real, I needed to generate income other ways (most authors don't make real money, by the way). As the universe would have it, the week after I committed to prioritizing connection, adventure, and freedom in my post-Pause life, I got an email from the Gates Foundation. An old team member was going on maternity leave. They needed someone to backfill the role for nine months. *Perfect—a familiar job I can do, with people I know.* It would provide money and a sense of stability as I continued to navigate the transition out of my Pause. I let them know I would need to work remotely (not typical pre-COVID-19) and shockingly, it looked like a green light. Informally people were already talking as if I had the job. All signs pointed toward me returning to where I had left, but policy required I go through an interview process.

I was interviewing with my old colleagues—many of whom I hadn't spoken with since the Great Pause. I'd already done the job—for YEARS—and VERY SUCCESSFULLY. I knew what I needed to say to pass the formality of the interview process.

While my head knew the drill, my heart was crying out to be seen. So, sister, this is what happened in the interview.

I talked about my goal of writing a book.

I talked about my new passion for rest, play, and Pauses.

I talked about the baby seeds of Soulcation.

I talked about how I was doing post-death, post-divorce, and post-departure.

I talked about the NEW ME, including all the parts that had nothing to do with driving forward the advocacy agenda of the Bill & Melinda Gates Foundation.

Despite years of training, I couldn't hold back. I was bursting at the seams. Everything that was once dormant in my soul—driving me to panic on the bathroom floor that rainy day three years ago—flowed out of me unabashed, unleashed, and untethered. I don't recommend this interview approach to anyone. When asked questions like "What do you want?" and "Where do you see yourself in five years?" I couldn't say what they wanted to hear. Instead, I said what I NEEDED to hear.

A few days later I got the call. "Mel, we know you can do this job. And we adore you. But we sense there are other things calling you right now. We've decided to go with another candidate."

A*nother candidate*? This job was dependent on relationships, ones that I HAD and spent over a decade building. There was no one better than me for the role. *Or was there?*

The old me was perfect for this role. But deep down the NEW ME was craving something NEW. Looking back, it's no surprise I came out unfiltered in the interviews. I had changed. I had done the inner work to undo the parts of me that were inauthentic. I had stripped away the filters and unpacked the conditioning that had once kept me safe. Authentic ME had found her way to the surface. My Grand Pause, with all its winding, invisible inner passages, hadn't been for nothing. I had turned inward, and now it was time to let things shift on the outside.

WHAT IF THERE IS NO RIGHT WAY?

We all know the feeling of a door being shut on our dreams. It can leave us with a shitload of self-doubt about whether we will ever be able to have what we want. In my case, I didn't get a job. Perhaps you've been fired or dumped or denied vacation time from a boss you swear is out to get you. It feels like the end of the world because in some ways, it *is* the end of the world you've consistently been imagining for yourself. The story that has been on repeat in your head for how things will play out has shattered into a million pieces. And this door slamming requires a subsequently new—and often unexpected—action from us: to rewrite another story.

If we're not careful, this new story can become infused with self-criticism. We beat ourselves up for all the time or money we poured into something that didn't work out. We cease trusting our desires. We make ourselves out to be a victim. We chastise ourselves for not seeing this coming. And worst of all, we might walk ourselves back from desiring whatever it was we wanted again. A closed door can spiral us into playing small and taming our desires, even though as we know through the Soulcation FUN-work, our happiness depends on us unleashing and pursuing our desires.

The stories that don't work out are the universe's way of calling us back to a story that is more authentically *us*.

When I was reckoning with my own abrupt closed door at the Gates Foundation, my friend Sarah flew out to be with me and asked me a powerful question.

"Mel, what if there was no right way?"

"Well, Sarah," I said. "I guess if there was no right way, I wouldn't have to get this whole job thing right on the first try. I wouldn't be in so much of a rush. Success could be soft and easy, rather than something with such a high bar only the luckiest or hardest working are rewarded with."

I sat in silence for a moment and then went on, "If there was no right way, I could be safe and belong even amidst an ocean of uncertainty. I could make a major career transition by looking for the next yellow arrow, like I learned to do while walking the Camino. There would be no need for a grand plan. I could rewrite a new plan because at the end of the day, there would be no right answer, only forward motion."

Sarah smiled, and when I was done she looked deep into my eyes and said, "There is only one version of success that matters, Mel, and that is the version that makes you feel exactly how you want to feel, on YOUR terms, with the stories YOU choose, and with a path to success that feels most like love, not struggle."

As I let her words sink in, I realized she was right. *Why would I want to live in a world where success was defined any other way?*

I could no longer go back to the Gates Foundation. That door was closed. Thankfully, I had all my Soulcation FUN-work tools to manage my feelings. I could feel panic, but I didn't need an emergency room anymore. I knew how to move through this emotional tunnel so the sadness didn't stay stuck inside. I could hear the sensations in my body clearly sending me a message: "Mel, it's time for a story with more human connection, more adventure, and more freedom. This is not just a Pause. You can't go back to your old life. You're safe to choose an entirely new lifestyle."

As I stared yet again at the rejection email from the Gates Foundation, Lisa's words popped back in my mind: "*What if you thought about this not as choosing a job, but choosing the deepest things you love?*"

That's when I knew, what felt most like love was an entirely new career. One where I was my own boss and took the helm of the brand I believed in the most: the Mel Miles brand. I didn't have any training in marketing. I knew very few entrepreneurs. I had no connections in the media or publishing industries. I didn't have a social media following. But I had a sense that I was supposed to build my own business—a business that felt like love.

A few weeks later, I got the word "free" tattooed on my arm and that evening, filed for my own LLC. It was time to let things shift and claim the Soulcation way of being as a longer-term way of life.

CHAPTER 13: FREE TO BE ME

I am holding hands with strangers in a musty church basement in Nashville, Tennessee. I hadn't been to church since my marriage ended. But I had returned for a meeting: Co-Dependents Anonymous, or CODA. I walked myself to the musty smelling basement as a commitment to myself. I wanted to sober up from my addiction to codependency, and like recovering from any addiction (but particularly one so subtle and so celebrated in society) I knew it would require consistent action.

It had been four months since I left Tel Aviv, Israel and returned to the U.S. I still didn't have a job, but I had a new hometown—Nashville. I needed *somewhere* to land (moving locations every month or so had become exhausting) and I'd heard the town was artsy, creative, and not too busy. So my Grand Pause ended with me filling two shopping carts at Target and renting a little craftsman house on the east side of the city. The day I moved, an acquaintance left a warm apple pie on my doorstep. I thought I had landed in heaven.

Nashville represented the hope of creating an ordinary yet deliciously happy life. For most of my adulthood, I had associated happiness with an extraordinary life: full of influence, wealth, fast-paced days, and loads of social events. But I didn't want these things anymore. My Pause had helped me reclaim the power and energy I'd slowly given away to religion, patriarchy, work, family, and my social networks—all at the expense of myself. On Soulcation, I had tasted the sweetness of a slow, spacious life. I didn't want to go back to busy. And I was here in Nashville to experiment with whether I could recreate the feelings of contentment and joy I felt on my

Pause in my everyday life. I wanted to try working in a different way. I wanted to see if I could build a company that impacted lives while also providing me enough time for rest, ease, and play that I wouldn't be counting the days until vacation. I had committed to giving it a try, but in just a few months in Nashville, I had already seen my old habits of working to the brink of exhaustion kick into gear. Holding hands with these strangers at this CODA meeting was my lifeline to support me in integrating the new Soulcation way.

There I was, in the circle, reciting the serenity prayer:

God, grant me the Serenity
to accept the things I cannot change,
Courage to change the things I can,
And Wisdom to know the difference.

I left the CODA meeting and headed to the parking lot, to get into my *new* car—another symbol of my commitment to building a life in Nashville. I looked down at my arm, still wrapped in bandages from my "FREE" tattoo Sarah had flown into town to watch me get. I had told her I didn't feel fully free yet, but it was the core desired feeling I wanted more than anything else in the world.

"Mel, sometimes you have to believe something first, before it can become a reality," she said to me when we walked through the doors of the east side tattoo parlor. I hoped like hell she was right.

HOW YOU CHANGE YOUR LIFE

Looking back on my own Pause, it started because I didn't want to collapse on the Gates Foundation bathroom floor ever again.

But perhaps like you, for years before I slowed down, I longed for healing and relief. It wasn't from a lack of desire that my life didn't change in all that time. It was because I was using the wrong formula for change. I was putting all my energy into changing my external actions instead of going inward to examine my internal beliefs.

I now believe Sarah was right. *You must believe something is true and act as if it is true long before it really will be true.* This is why step "U" (Unlearn Limiting Beliefs) from the Soulcation FUN-work is essential to living a life you don't need a vacation from. You change your life when you change your beliefs about yourself and your desires. In turn, these new beliefs will change your actions (for example, doing something on your Happy List every single morning). And these new actions, practiced consistently on a daily basis, can change your life.

Too many women chronically suffer from burnout and anxiety for years. They find little relief because they haven't been taught the tools that help them change their inner beliefs about themselves, which in turn will change their future. Soul-Scripting is one of those tools. It's the process of getting really clear on what you want, and what beliefs you will embody when you are that person living in your desired future state. It's similar to manifesting but focused on imagination and sensations far more than the mind and thought. In fact, you don't have to think something is possible to Soul-Script. You just need *to connect with the feeling of it being possible, long before you take any action.* For example, I had to get the tattoo that said "free" before I felt free. I had to envision myself as a business owner before I took the action of filing for an LLC. Connecting with this future self is the fastest way I've found to change our beliefs.

My own Soul-Scripting practice was birthed through the coaching and teaching of Emily Hazel, known as Spirited Seeker online. She defines it this way:

> *"{Soul} Scripting is essentially the screenplay of your future that you create with intention. It's a sacred document, a love letter, a magical manifesto that supports your wishes, ideas and desires to come to fruition through a practice of reading and* embodying *the life of your dreams. Rather than cruising along with life not really ever considering that you CAN experience all the things you wish to experience and feeling disheartened* (or worse, in despair*) that you can't have what you want, this practice invites you - actually,* demands you - *take responsibility for your life, your actions, your emotionality, your wellbeing and your stories."*[20]

We spend a lot of time rolling around questions like "What if it goes wrong?" in our heads. I get it. When it comes to our biggest dreams and goals, we all have voices in our heads telling us, "I'll never get there," or "I can't get there fast enough" or even "Why even try?" Yet when we think, "I don't have enough ______________________________ (time/money/relationships/opportunity)," we create a belief block that keeps us living in a scarcity mindset. Soul-Scripting is so powerful because it reverses this belief block and helps unlocks a new mindset.

How does it work? Here are the steps I walk my clients through in my Soulcation group coaching program:

- Imagine your future dreams/goals in areas of your life you want to shift. I usually write to these categories: work, pleasure/play, health, family, friendships, and romance.
- Write them out as if they already happened. Use words that feel luscious. Connect with the emotion. Imagine yourself, there in the exact moment you are longing for.
- Write the story in the present tense.
- Record it as a voice memo and listen to it daily as you get ready or when you're on the go (or if you are a paper person—print it out and put it somewhere you will see and can read daily). Let it serve as a portal to access your core desired feelings and experiment with new narratives about your life.

Curious what this looks like? Here is an example from my 2020 Soul-Script on the topic that I arguably wanted more than anything else in life—a new romantic partner:

> *My body feels light, like I'm floating on the water without any concern of drifting too far. I don't feel like I need to be in the same room as my partner to feel his energy and love. It's always there—soothing my anxious tendencies and reminding me I can be still, playful, and feminine. He speaks words of truth over me, and I know deep in my bones and flesh he's not going anywhere. In our relationship, I feel secure, like a kite that can be blown by the wind but always has a strong anchor holding me on land: free but tethered. Wild but safe all at the same time.*
>
> *Our relationship has clear guardrails and boundaries, but a deep knowledge that we are each choosing the other person and in that choosing, day after day, is where the*

magic happens. Inside the cocoon of our relationship, I feel safe and warm. I get held by his strong, inviting arms all through the night—letting the touch vibrate through me into the deepest, most subconscious parts of me, transmitting love. The energy we have is emotional, not just physical. Sparks of emotional connection started long before we ever experienced physical intimacy, and we have built an energy around this emotional fluidity.

I bask in the gift of being fully seen by him, without needing to offer anything in return. He listens to my feelings, desires, and needs. He is up for both spontaneous adventures and slow, simple days, and openly shares his own inner world and inner knowing with me. He has done the hard work to heal the wounds of his past, faced his ego and integrated the masculine and feminine. His mind is sharp, and he has access to a deep well of soul knowledge, which he freely gives in support of my own work. He shows up for me fully HERE—in his body, in the present moment, with full surrender to any outcome.

He fucks me soft and slow, and I come to him with no fear of performance or attachment to an orgasmic outcome. Our sex life is an explorative journey, and it creates an energetic bond between us that activates a passion and creativity for all dimensions of life. We dance through the world together, independently moving to our own steps but connected by the same beat. He is my harmony, my partner for life, because I choose him, and he chooses me.

For my entire life up until I wrote this, my body and mind only knew what it was like to be in a toxic romantic partnership. I didn't have a mental model for an emotionally connected, healthy container. In fact, during my Pause I frequently doubted I'd ever have more than breadcrumbs from men. This Soul-Script is what helped me break through my limiting belief. The desire I had to be reconnected with another man besides Brock, in an entirely different way, could no longer stay a distant thought. It became tactile, detailed, and specific, no longer lingering in the realm of "someday, maybe." It was conscious, clear, and directional. And after a few months of listening to it out loud, I could feel myself ready to date in an entirely different way.

Sisters, this is the power of Soul-Scripting. When we name our dreams and bring them to the surface, we really turn our mind, and then our life, in an entirely different direction.

TRUST THE WINDS OF LIFE

Wind and sea salt whipped through my hair. I was standing at the bow of the sailboat, looking down at water so clear I could see fish swimming down below. My phone had been off for seven full days, the result of a spontaneous decision to sign up to go sailing with seven strangers through the British Virgin Islands.

I had been feeling the stress of integrating into my life post-Pause. Starting a business, finding clients, and integrating into a more structured life was testing me. I knew I needed to clear my head. If I was going to dedicate years of my life to something as big as Soulcation, I needed to know deep in my core it was a Hell YES. So, with the last bit of money in my Pause savings account, I booked this sailing trip. The stakes were high. We were strangers from five different countries and very different backgrounds. We had to live together in close quarters, sail in high winds, cook for each other, sleep and rise together, and even coordinate flushing our toilets at sea. It wasn't always comfortable, but it forced me to adapt each day's goals and destination by the wind. My mind slowed down, and in the silence, I found the noise and angst I was feeling about my new company melt away.

When I returned to land and turned on my phone again, I rapidly typed out this message to my friends. It was titled, "my decision-making process" and it said:

> *Sometimes the best thing we can do is open ourselves up to new people. To let them pass through our lives without expectations or agenda, but with curiosity and a soft invitation to let them change us.*
>
> *Sometimes we need new ideas and new perspectives, and the only way toward newness is choosing an adventure not everyone understands.*
>
> *Sometimes we don't have to try so hard in relationships. We can let the earthy, physical acts of surviving pull us closer—like hoisting sails or searching the open waters for a lost dinghy or cooking on a stove that sways with the ocean waves.*
>
> *Sometimes in life you need to read a book and ask wise mentors for advice. But sometimes you need to leave all the advice behind and say yes to slowness and silence—*

because in letting go of control you actually find yourself more fully.

Sometimes we don't need to be chasing a forever goal. We just need to be creating space in our hearts. Inviting the unexpected. Trusting the currents we feel against our back. Welcoming strangers into our life.

And sometimes these strangers will bring you a unicorn costume and literally pull you to shore. They will find a tiny island in the middle of the sea. They will dance with you under tropical rain, teach you how to do the limbo with a horn, pour you rum until the moon sets and the sky fills with a million stars, and make sure you know that people from all walks of life can hold you in love.

It was one of the best weeks of my life—and I finally trust the wind that is carrying me to a new place.

My friends, don't forget the currents of life can be trusted—and there is an abundance of love out there for our taking.

CHAPTER 14: AWAKENING THE WILD WOMAN WITHIN

I was starting to settle into Nashville. However, the people I was meeting kept asking me, "Mel, do you want to go to church with me on Sunday?" I wanted social connections more than anything, but I knew deep down I had changed my religious beliefs. The very system I grew up in I didn't want to go back to, and I had a deep feeling of peace. I felt God in the world around me. A wild woman didn't want to be tamed in the church pews.

SCALING THE FREEDOM LADDER

The word FREE was tattooed on my arm, and I was committed to designing a life that felt free. Yet as I sat in my new coworking space in Nashville and engaged in friendly chit chat, I noticed conversations always gravitated to the *stressors* of life. Where was all the talk about the *joys* of life? I wanted to make Nashville work, and on some level, I wanted to be friends with all the busy entrepreneurs I was meeting. But even more than that, I wanted to be happy.

I thought back to the happiest women I met during my Pause. Women I believed embodied freedom, and who inspired me to believe in the Soulcation way of life. I opened my laptop and typed an email asking them to answer this question in any manner they chose: "What does it mean to you to be free?"

Samantha from New Zealand responded back immediately and wrote, "Alive in the world as my most true and authentic self."

Helena from France said, "The ability to fully realize myself." Ruth from Zimbabwe shared, "Financial freedom to spend time on the things I want to do." Lilia from Canada's message said, "...to travel abundantly, to love freely, to live in a place that brings joy, to explore this wild earth, and to have time to pursue life's passions." My favorite response was from Josie in Argentina:

> *{Freedom means}... swimming across a vast expanse of water or at the summit of a mountain in complete stillness or sitting on the rooftop of a car after skydiving with the love of my life. It's essentially that feeling you get when you are fully present in the moment and time feels, momentarily, suspended.*

All these women were far along on their own Soulcation paths, and their responses displayed for me conceptions of freedom that were as diverse as I believe freedom ought to be. They also showed me a definition of freedom that was layered, malleable, and as complex as my own personal struggle to break out of the cage and find it. Freedom is not present or absent. It is on a continuum. When we see it as binary, say we have it, and stop chasing a deeper form of freedom, I think we stop living in some way. We curtail our growth and miss out on the pleasure of making the pursuit of freedom a lifetime sport.

This journey of uncovering more freedom is the essence of Soulcation. We are free when we know in our innermost being we can always, no matter how far we've traveled in life, change our mind, our beliefs, and our relationships any time we need to. And we get to this full expression of freedom through what I call the **Freedom Ladder**. It involves fours steps: Physical Freedom, Social Freedom, Inner Freedom, and finally, the pinnacle of self-realization, Wild Freedom.

To ascend this ladder, two things are needed. First, admit the parts of you that don't feel free yet; second, connect with a future version of yourself that is more free (which you can do in your Soul-Script).

Physical Freedom

The first results that come up in Webster's dictionary for freedom define it in a physical sense:

> *"{Freedom}: the absence of necessity, coercion, or constraint in choice or action"* and *"liberation from slavery or restraint or from the power of another."*[21]

It's our human right to be physically safe and liberated, and this foundation is needed for any of us to move up the Freedom Ladder. Unfortunately, in many countries, basic freedom is still a struggle. According to the Human Freedom Index Report published in 2020 (the most comprehensive global assessment of rule of law, safety, expression of religion, property rights, financial stability, and more), the overall level of freedom decreased in seventy countries.[22] This means a growing proportion of people are still lacking basic freedoms. It's a tragic equity and human rights problem, and what originally led me to choose a career in international development. I believe investments in both advocacy and direct aid are urgently needed, and I dedicate my own time and charitable dollars to be part of the solutions.

In fact, as someone privileged enough to be born with significant Physical Freedom, I've noticed over the course of my life when I am not participating in an effort to advance Physical Freedom for others, my energy across all areas of life dwindles. Deep gratitude for our Physical Freedom is in itself a birthplace of joy.

Social Freedom

The second way freedom is defined is in regard to how we think about what is expected of us.

> *"{Freedom}: the quality or state of being exempt or released usually from something onerous."*[23]

Women in particular are quite good at tolerating difficulty and "onerous" situations. We take on invisible tasks outside our job description, do most of the emotional labor at home, and still feel guilty for spending money on ourselves. We've been conditioned by generations of ancestral and patriarchal messages that *life is hard*. "That's just the way things are," we've been told. We're expected not to question our roles, or heaven forbid, demand task-shifting to relieve some of the pressure. We think the only way to fight back is to play by the rules handed down to us and prove we can manage the difficulty. The belief that life could be easy never occurs to us. We never stop to consider if success could come by choosing the path of ease and lightness, rather than struggle. We juggle all the balls and take on onerous tasks because we doubt we can choose what feels good and still belong. But a life that feels like constant struggle isn't a life of complete freedom. Freedom is being released from anything onerous. When we adopt the Soulcation practice of giving ourselves permission to let go of things, people, jobs, tasks, or otherwise onerous parts of our life, we open a path to evolve to the next level of our human experience: Inner Freedom.

Inner Freedom

"{Freedom}: the quality of being frank, open, or outspoken"[24]

This stage of the Freedom Ladder unlocks not only significant improvements in your relationship to self, but also begins to unlock your power to create and change the world. In this phase, you know what you want and are not afraid to ask for it. Using your voice to speak your desires, anger, grief, feelings, and needs is a grand act of freedom. No longer are you saying what others want to hear or abiding by what will be accepted. You don't stay on script to protect your sense of worthiness or belonging. You are now a woman on a mission. You have divisive opinions. You offend people. You don't mess around. You aren't afraid to use your voice to call people out and say uncomfortable things. You know at the end of the day, you're not responsible for other people's feelings. You're responsible for honoring your truth. You know the rewards of freedom are worth the risk of not belonging. (Because heck, belonging to a community that edits your voice doesn't sound that fun anyway.) And most of all, as you use your voice to call out all barriers, inequities, and patriarchal wounding in women's way, you not only help yourself, but also help other women on their own freedom journeys. Eventually, as you use your voice in bigger and bigger ways, you will start to see this Inner Freedom birth new life and happiness inside you. Your voice becomes your engine for connection, creativity, and change. You have secured Physical Freedom, Social Freedom, Inner Freedom, and you are climbing the ladder to one of the deepest layers of freedom: Wild Freedom.

Wild Freedom

"{Freedom}: boldness of conception or execution"[25]

This is the step where you awaken the wild woman within. You roar. You play like when you were a child. You live from a Happy List. You stand on your own two feet. You speak clear, wholehearted "yeses" and "noes." You dance—sometimes naked under the stars in your backyard—just because you can. You demand slow, passionate love from your lovers, because you know that is the best kind. You walk through the world knowing deep down in your bones you are free: free to try something new. Free to wander. Free to not know where you're going. Free to be lost for a good long while. Free to Pause and then start a new career or make a new home. Free to challenge authority and question beliefs. Free to stay or leave. Free to befriend and then unfriend. Free to turn your back or open your heart, whenever you want. You may be called a heretic, but you are actually one of the lucky ones who is wild and free. No matter what happens, you know without a shadow of a doubt no one can ever take away from you your Wild Freedom, because you have done the inner work to set yourself free.

Climbing up the four stages on the Freedom Ladder is the process of being human. No one gets a fast pass. Not even the billionaires. (I promise, I've worked for two.) We all have to do the work. We must acknowledge the ways we still don't feel physically, socially, inwardly, or wildly free in life.

Soulcation is our way toward change.

Each person will have their own sticking points. In my experience, it often takes years to peel each layer back. That's entirely okay. And that's also the point. We never arrive at a box called "free" we can check off. Freedom is the feeling you get inside when you know you are changing, evolving, becoming, and best of all, when you sense you're onto something good.

Sister, my dream for you is to live in a world where you feel free to do whatever your heart wants to do. Your heart will always be calling you home to deeper layers of Physical, Social, Inner, and Wild Freedom. It's your job to follow it. That's when you know you're on Soulcation.

THE SOULCATION MANIFESTO

If something isn't working, switch it up. I now believe this is the best advice I can give anyone longing for more freedom. You can always switch things up. You can change your mind, religion, opinion, and ultimately, your entire life. I hope my path serves as an example. I spent years building credibility in a career I've since shifted away from. I left a religion. I thought my entire life I wanted to be a mother, and now, I'm open to never birthing a child myself.

You can always switch things up.

BUT, MEL, HOW?

I hope this book has offered you a new way—the Soulcation way—to create space, go inward, and connect with your intuitive "how." But when in doubt, remember this:

When women stop trying so damned hard to be good, we can finally be free.

We can't be free when we're in constant service or striving mode. Human hearts speak on a wavelength only accessible to one another when we're not in a hurry. Yet for decades, women have moved at lightning speed, whispering, "I'm so worn out," to their people late at night, then waking up the next morning to another set of appointments, lists, and demands. Sister, your soul is knocking on the door of your life, inviting you to come alive and swim in the ocean of freedom. You soul has dreams to dance under the stars, make wild love, and design a life you don't need a vacation from.

I've written this book because I believe in a world where women radically and powerfully choose themselves, and in doing so, find their life overflowing with love and freedom—the real, juicy, safe kind that doesn't require any action to keep flowing. Pleasure is your birthright and it's ripe for your taking if you're brave enough to surrender into the softness of the Soulcation way. If you're ready to say yes to a Soulcation, I invite you to go to takeasoulcation.com for further resources and offerings.

I'll leave you with this manifesto, which I read to each woman in my group coaching program.

Soulcation Manifesto

We believe it's for freedom that we are set free.

We acknowledge we miss out on life when we lead with our calculating mind and neglect the still, soft nudges of our hearts.

When in doubt, we turn inward—toward our higher power and ourselves—rather than outward to a world full of noise and life hacks for how to fix our lives.

We make every effort to accept the unknown, and by doing so, grant ourselves the freedom to change our minds, opinions, and beliefs along the way.

We refuse to abandon ourselves for the sake of approval, status, or love. We will show up each day as our true selves, knowing this is the only way we can truly be free.

We use our voice and take up space in the world, without apology.

We believe that true knowing is not about figuring everything out in our heads. It's about learning to trust what rings true in our hearts.

We give ourselves tremendous grace, knowing we are doing the most difficult work of our lives. We celebrate being in process—not arriving.

We believe the rules do not apply; we make our way through the darkness by walking.

We pursue self-care with reckless abandon and are shameless about loving and tending to our souls.

We commit to show up as our real, messy selves: unmasked, unfiltered, and untamed.

We acknowledge most of the time that our biggest critics are ourselves, and we work hard to silence the inner critics, for that is the path to inner freedom.

EPILOGUE

The sun is setting over the Caribbean Sea, filling the sky with pinks and oranges. It is my thirty-fourth birthday, the age that classifies me as "geriatric" when it comes to Western pregnancies. But I'm not thinking about the goal of having kids, or buying that house, or even what will come of my new business. I'm right here, barefoot, and sandy-toed, staring up at the glow of a full moon. My body is filled with the sensations of ease, and I can't help but think to myself, "Mel, you've arrived exactly where you've always wanted to be: here on the beach, in your body, in the present moment ... living fully alive."

I look across the table at the faces of twenty souls. Men and women from all over the world, who have come together to spend six weeks together in Playa del Carmen, Mexico. I met them only a week ago, but they are throwing a birthday party for me tonight. We eat all the shrimp tacos we can, then move closer to the water's edge. Tequila shots are poured. The song "Dancing in the Moonlight" plays through the speakers. My body is fluid, hips swaying and head flipping in circles. All my tight muscles, creaky joints, and stress acne from my corporate days are gone. After doing the deep inner work of Soulcation I finally feel untethered, wild, and free.

The dancing continues, and I look at Sara with a smirk.

"What, Mel?" she says as she grabs my hand to spin me around on our beach dance floor.

"You know what?" I say, "It's time for starnuding." For those not yet familiar with the deeply spiritual hobby of starnuding, I define it as the art of swimming naked under the stars, with the intention of being in your body, feeling the softness of the water, and taking in the vastness of the stars. I swear starnuding is equivalent to a therapy session. It makes you feel calm and held by something bigger than yourself.

"Let's try to rally the group," I say. "You know this is exactly what I want for my birthday."

We move everyone a little further down the beach to a place without lights. Then Sara and I strip down, letting our pale naked bodies stand out in the darkness. I scream, "Y'all, it's freedom hour!!!" at the top of my lungs and everyone turns. We run naked into the water and gaze up at the stars in amazement, bodies emersed in calming softness.

"Come on, everyone!" I scream again from the water. "It feels amazing."

Somewhat to my surprise, everyone follows. The advertising guy from New York. The shy tech founder from London. The jokester from Switzerland. And the smattering of souls ranging from twenty-five years old to fifty. Everyone leaves their clothes in a pile on the shore and plunges into the water: naked and unashamed.

We tread water and look up. "There are a million stars above us. This is magical," someone says.

"Holy crap, this is awesome. I can't believe how big the moon is," another chimes in.

We chat some, but mostly we float in silence, letting our bodies come into the fullness of presence and pleasure of the night sky, the warmth of the sea, and the privilege to be naked, held, and happy.

"This is fully living," I say to myself. I'm thirty-four and surrounded by the love of the universe. Not the ordinary type of love or the kind that can come and go with other humans, but the extraordinary, universal kind of love that's available to everyone, everywhere, once you're willing to strip your life naked and surrender to it.

My trip to Playa del Carmen, Mexico was supposed to be six weeks. But nearly nine months later, I haven't left. I am writing the final words of this book from a beachfront café in "Playa." The world has radically changed due to COVID-19, as has my life. Playa del Carmen is a town most people only come to for vacation, but I now call this small beach town my home. Three years ago, I set out on Soulcation in a state of emotional overwhelm and burnout. On the other side, I've designed a life that includes the things I used to only let myself do on vacation in my everyday life. It's proof that when you commit to the Soulcation way, you CAN design a life you don't need a vacation from. It just takes radical willingness to begin again—over and over, as many times as you need—along the way.

Nashville didn't work out. I was there for a year, living by the Soulcation framework and making strides at building community, the Soulcation business, and a new life. Over that year, I sat in hours of traffic, attended the circuit of Nashville concerts, and went on too many coffee dates where the conversations gravitated toward what I call the "vortex of next" (your next kid, next house, next job, and yes, next vacation). Despite the external charm and welcome of the South, my anxiety came back, and my skin broke out in acne. I knew by then my body was telling me something was more deeply out of alignment.

The truth was, I wanted a bamboo treehouse in Bali, not some U.S. city. I wanted to spend my evenings listening to the sound of the waves on the beach, not in traffic or in front of a screen. I wanted to call up a friend and say, "Meet me in fifteen minutes," rather than exchange four emails to schedule dinner two weeks out. I wanted to live in a community with new voices passing in and out, rather than claw my way into what felt like already established circles. Things were getting real—and difficult. I was struggling to find people, purpose, and yes, a lover who aligned with my core values of freedom, adventure, and travel. Then one day while walking the aisles at Target, I had a scary thought: I wanted a vacation from my Nashville world.

I was my own boss. I had traversed my dark emotional tunnels, healed my panic disorder, and pivoted my lifestyle to prioritize happiness. I had recently come up with what is now the tagline for Soulcation: "Design a life you don't need a vacation from." It wasn't "design a life that feels good eighty percent of the time," or "design a life where you have more vacation time than anyone else," or even "design a life that is more than tolerable." I was building a company to spread the message that women can shatter the patriarchy and truly design a life they didn't need a vacation from. I believed it. But I was also being called more deeply into it.

I had bought all new furniture, signed a lease, and told everyone I knew, "I have officially moved to Nashville." I felt obligated to plant my feet firmly in this life choice, one that I had spent a year wandering the globe and most of my life savings to arrive at. Nashville was serving me as an entrepreneur. How could I leave? That's when I heard the words of sweet Susan in my mind: "If something isn't working, switch it up."

I went home that night and pulled out my stack of journals. I found the one where I wrote my very first Happy List that day at Willows Lodge. My body remembered the sensation of being under water in the bathtub, contemplating if I should just not come up. I looked down at the list, crafted from a time of despair. I had completed EVERYTHING. All the far-off places, wild dreams, and little splurges. Everything I had told myself, "I wonder if ___ would help," I had said yes to. I gave myself permission to be both experimental and extravagant with my own life. I started living by my Happy List, and it literally saved my life.

I had done everything on the original list. I had fulfilled a dream, and in the pursuit of the dream, healed the pain, panic, and anxiety caused by my suppressed desires. I was at the end of a grand journey, and in my arriving, I was losing my inner mojo. This is what was wrong!

Yes, I had my morning routine and daily time for play and rest. Yet in my post-Target existential soul-searching, it clicked. I didn't have another big dream. I was still casting too small a vision for what was possible for my life. I needed to refresh my Happy List and claim a new set of adventures, activities, and radical acts of self-love that would keep my flame for life alive. After all, it appeared that without this—I would settle for a life that sometimes (including during trips to Target), I would want to escape from.

So right there, in my bedroom in Nashville, I wrote this new list.

Soulcation Happy List

- Move to a beach town with a slower pace. End every workday on the ocean shore, listening to the waves
- Buy a sustainable bamboo house connected to nature for indoor/outdoor living and retreats
- Learn to salsa and make dance a consistent part of my life
- Learn to surf
- Learn to fluently speak Spanish and Portuguese
- Learn to scuba dive
- Learn to sail, then go sail in Greece, Tahiti, and Mexico

- Lead Soulcation retreats with small groups of six to eight women in amazing destinations around the world
- Visit Morocco and experience a local hammam
- Sleep in dome tents under the Northern Lights in Iceland
- Soak in natural thermal hot springs and hike in northern Italy
- Climb Mt. Kilimanjaro
- Complete yoga teacher training
- Attend my first Vipassana meditation retreat
- Own a designer wardrobe and find pleasure in getting dressed each morning
- Go to the airport and buy a ticket to somewhere, day of

It was a Soulcation list of possibility. A version written by an entirely different person than the one in the Willows Lodge bathtub. And since I already knew about the life-changing magic of a Happy List, I was ready to go all-in.

LIVING WHERE MOST PEOPLE ONLY GO ON VACATION

My new Happy List served as my North Star for decision-making. I read it to myself each morning and connected to the feeling of freely traveling, working, dating, and going about my daily life in places most people only went on vacation. I envisioned myself walking on a white sandy beach each morning, doing mission-driven work from a bamboo house, and embodying the slow, lazy vibe my soul so desperately craved.

Some of the things on my Happy List would not be cheap. I no longer had a savings account to dip into. If I was going to make this work, I knew I'd need to get creative. It didn't take much budgeting to know I couldn't fly from Nashville to the beach every other weekend. Yet, I could live in a beach town outside the U.S. with a much lower cost of living. I couldn't afford fancy vacations to Bali or Italy, but I could probably afford to be there if I didn't have a mortgage or rent back in the U.S. I didn't have a lot of cash for all the lessons and trainings I wanted to invest in, but I did own a relatively new car I could sell and use the cash to learn what I wanted to learn. I didn't own more than one swimsuit, but I knew I'd have much better luck finding the beachy wardrobe and sparkly swimsuits of my dreams if I was in a town with what my heart was craving most: WATER.

Yet again I took a leap and officially moved to Mexico. My adopted hometown of Playa del Carmen has inspired my creativity, elevated my joy, and made me more alive than ever in my life. I don't set an alarm. I wake up to a balcony that overlooks palm trees and the bright yellows and reds of Mexico's architecture. I run my businesses from dreamy garden patios and outdoor cafes, eating shrimp tacos and acai bowls for a few dollars each. I end each workday exactly where I dreamed: on the ocean shore, listening to the waves roll gently onto the sand, reminding me we are made to float with the currents of life, rather than swim upstream in resistance. I spend my evenings in connection with a diverse community of nomads from all over the world who, just like me, showed up here knowing no one, but are willing to speak their truth, open their hearts, and say yes to my spontaneous, "Margarita in 15 mins?" texts. I spent the pandemonium of Christmas 2020 eating fresh fish in a tiny town called El Cuyo, off the grid, safe, and happy. I have learned to scuba dive. I have sailed. I completed this book, including writing the first draft in four months (which in book world is lightning speed). My list of dreams is being birthed into reality. And while I know I'll need to keep adding things to my Happy List, I have embodied the essence of Soulcation.

Mexico may not be home forever, but it will always be one of my most life-changing homes because it convinced me that when I honor what I want, then find a way to generate income, then cultivate aligned community, I really can design a life I don't need a vacation from. You don't need to start from a place of strength to unlock this happiness. I didn't. The key is to do the work to remember who you truly are and what you really want. This, soul sisters, is the life-saving magic of Soulcation.

ACKNOWLEDGEMENTS

When I decided to write this book, I found myself turning to the acknowledgements section of every book I picked up. I was coming up against my own limiting beliefs about being a creative woman. I needed to be reminded that every book—just like every dream—takes a village to birth into existence.

I started this journey without one contact in publishing. I didn't know a single published author. I had no knowledge of how to write non-fiction, let alone market and sell it. All I had was a yearning inside of me to put words on a page and my Happy List notepad from my stay at Willows Lodge with the words "write a book" scribbled on it.

I started my writing journey only six months after my divorce. I was deeply grieving the plans my ex-husband and I had to start a family. I knew I wasn't likely going to birth a child anytime soon, so I decided I'd birth a book instead. Like any birth process, there was stretching, growing pains, night sweats, and frantic calls for help. Soulcation is now my book baby, and I couldn't be a prouder mama about what I birthed into creation.

For those reading this, I hope it's a testament to the truth that we can do hard things, but we need to take the time to build (sometimes from ground zero like I did) the webs of community and connection that will facilitate the dreams of our heart.

To Ally Fallon, who invited me into her living room weeks after I left the Gates Foundation and helped me map out my memoir. I carried those book notecards around the world with me, and while I never ended up publishing the memoir, it's the book I needed to write to become the woman who has found her voice.

To my writing coach, Patti Hall. I couldn't have made it through this solo act without your gut reactions, technical critiques, and late-night texts cheering me on. My guest room is always here for you.

To the Unsettled and Hacker Paradise communities who taught me about a slower, more intentional, and playful way to live, our rhythms of life together changed me forever. You have convinced me people from all walks of life can pass through my life, dance in the rain with me, and hold me in love.

To the men who I've dated, who have offered me love, demonstrated a new way of being in relationships, and helped me become the sexually liberated, wild, and free woman I am today, thank you.

To my best friends, Sufey, Sarah, and Steff, who walked with me on this journey to free my soul. Thank you.

To the women who were there that sudden night my ex-husband left me (Rosalyn, Laura, and Heidi)—you held space for me on the hardest day of my life, and I am forever grateful.

To the Gates Foundation malaria team who sent me away with love, support, and the biggest surprise of my life. This book is my thank you.

To Abi—I didn't believe you when you told me to leap and the net shall appear, but you were right all along.

To Ashley—Soulcation's first employee and the copy editor behind these beautiful words, I couldn't have done it without you.

To my therapists and coaches, Lisa, Susan, Jay, and Jasmine, who taught me to reconnect with my emotions, my body, and my womb—thank you. I can only do this work because you were a safe witness as I journeyed back home to myself.

To the other authors I found via the internet, events, and Instagram who offered advice and support along the way, your wisdom meant the world. You were right: We can always change our career, learn something new, and bring new people into our life.

To my agent at the Bindery Agency, you respected I had changed my mind about my Christian faith, and honored my need to part ways. Thanks for teaching me about publishing and affirming the use of my most authentic voice no matter how it "lands" in the market.

To my friends and community in Mexico, who lived with me through the most historic year of our generation, you feel like family. You embodied love to me and witnessed me as I wrote all the words of this book.

To my dad, brother, and sister-in-law, who also had to do the brave work of redesigning life after Mom's death, I'm so glad we've had each other as we've figured out our Option B.

Finally, to my mother, who whispered across the living room days before she died, "Mel, you should write a book." Even in your physical absence, these words sent me on a journey that changed my life. You knew long before I did that writing would be my path to freedom.

ENDNOTES

1 “Any Anxiety Disorder.” National Institute of Mental Health, https://www.nimh.nih.gov/health/statistics/any-anxiety-disorder.

2 Anne Helen Petersen, *Can’t Even: How Millennials Became the Burnout Generation* (Boston: Houghton Mifflin Harcourt, 2020).

3 “CNBC|SurveyMonkey poll: International Women’s Day 2021,” SurveyMonkey, https://www.surveymonkey.com/curiosity/cnbc-women-at-work-2021/.

4 Emily Nagoski, PhD, and Amelia Nagoski, DMA, *Burnout: The Secret to Unlocking the Stress Cycle* (New York: Ballantine Books, 2019).

5 Emilia Roig. *Why We Matter*. 3 Auflage 2021.

6 Valerie Rein, PhD, *Patriarchy Stress Disorder: The Invisible Inner Barrier to Women’s Happiness and Fulfillment* (Lioncrest Publishing, 2019).

7 Claire Bidwell Smith, *Anxiety: The Missing Stage of Grief: A Revolutionary Approach to Understanding and Healing the Impact of Loss* (New York: Da Capo Press, 2018).

8 David Kessler, *Finding Meaning: The Sixth Stage of Grief* (New York: Scribner, 2019).

9 Thomas Merton, *Conjectures of a Guilty Bystander* (New York: Doubleday Religion, 1965).

10 “What is mindfulness?” Mindful.org, July 8, 2020, https://www.mindful.org/what-is-mindfulness/.

11 Robert Holden, PhD, *Loveability: Knowing How to Love and Be Loved* (Hay House Inc., 2014).

12 Derek Sivers, "If You're Not Feeling 'Hell Yeah!' Then Say No," https://sive.rs/hyn.
13 Mary Oliver, "Wild Geese" in *Dream Work* (The Atlantic Monthly Press, 1986).
14 Stuart Brown, *Play: How it Shapes the Brain, Opens the Imagination, and Invigorates the Soul* (New York: Penguin Group, 2009).
15 Bronnie Ware, *Top Five Regrets of the Dying: A Life Transformed by the Dearly Departing* (Hay House Inc., 2019).
16 David A. Frederick, H. Kate St. John, Justin R. Garcia, and Elisabeth A. Lloyd, "Differences in Orgasm Frequency Among Gay, Lesbian, Bisexual, and Heterosexual Men and Women in a U.S. National Sample, *Archives of Sexual Behavior* 47, 273-288 (2018). https://doi.org/10.1007/s10508-017-0939-z.
17 Joe Dispenza, *Breaking the Habit of Being Yourself: How to Lose Your Mind and Create a New One* (Hay House, Inc., 2012).
18 Judson Brewer, *Unwinding Anxiety: New Science Shows How to Break the Cycles of Worry and Fear to Heal Your Mind* (New York: Avery, Penguin Random House LLC, 2021).
19 Danielle LaPorte, *The Desire Map: A Guide to Creating Goals with Soul* (Sounds True, 2014).
20 Emily Hazel, "Scripting: Manifest What You Want Using This Practice," Spirited Seeker, https://spiritedseeker.com/read/scripting.
21 "Freedom." *Merriam-Webster.com Dictionary,* Merriam-Webster, https://www.merriam-webster.com/dictionary/freedom.

22 Ian Vásquez and Fred McMahon, *The Human Freedom Index 2020: A Global Measurement of Personal, Civil, and Economic Freedom* (Cato Institute and Fraser Institute, 2020).

23 "Freedom." *Merriam-Webster.com Dictionary,* Merriam-Webster, https://www.merriam-webster.com/dictionary/freedom.

24 "Freedom." *Merriam-Webster.com Dictionary,* Merriam-Webster, https://www.merriam-webster.com/dictionary/freedom.

25 "Freedom." *Merriam-Webster.com Dictionary,* Merriam-Webster, https://www.merriam-webster.com/dictionary/freedom.

Manufactured by Amazon.ca
Bolton, ON

25565531R00131